100+ pizza recipes. Pi
The most popular and easy pizza recipes

© Copyright 2018 by Amy Fincher - All rights reserved.

All rights Reserved. No part of this publication or the information in it may be quoted from or reproduced in any form by means such as printing, scanning, photocopying or otherwise without prior written permission of the copyright holder.

Disclaimer and Terms of Use: Effort has been made to ensure that the information in this book is accurate and complete, however, the author and the publisher do not warrant the accuracy of the information, text and graphics contained within the book due to the rapidly changing nature of science, research, known and unknown facts and internet. The Author and the publisher do not hold any responsibility for errors, omissions or contrary interpretation of the subject matter herein. This book is presented solely for motivational and informational purposes only.

INTRODUTION

Prepare your taste buds for well over 100 delectable pizza recipes. Contained in this book are recipes for anybody who like the pizza cooking.

Each recipe is complete with detailed cooking instructions. That way, you'll have as much fun cooking the dishes as you will eating them.

In this book you find more than 100 pizza recipes for any occasion.

«If you will like my book please leave your honest review about it on Amazon.com»

Best regards,

Amy Fincher «LuckyBooks»

TABLE OF CONTENTS

INTRODUCTION
1. SLOW-COOKER PIZZA
2. PRIMAVERA SKILLET PIZZA
3. ZUCCHINI PIZZA CRUST
4. GRILLED PIZZA BREAD
5. BBQ CHICKEN SKILLET PIZZA
6. LOW-CARB BREAKFAST PIZZA
7. MICKEY PIZZAS
8. EGG-IN-A-HOLE PIZZA BAGELS
9. CRUSTLESS PEPPERONI PIZZA
10. PICKLE PIZZA
11. CAPTAIN AMERICA PIZZA
12. CAULIFLOWER CRUST PIZZA
13. THE WORKS SKILLET PIZZA
14. HAM, EGG, & CHEESE BREAKFAST PIZZA
15. CAULIFLOWER BREAKFAST PIZZA
16. SAUSAGE CAULIFLOWER PIZZA
17. CORNBREAD BREAKFAST PIZZA
18. MINI DEEP-DISH PIZZAS
19. GLUTEN-FREE BROCCOLI CRUST PIZZA RECIPE
20. DEEP DISH CAULIFLOWER PIZZA
21. BBQ CHICKEN CRUST PIZZA
22. PIZZADILLAS
23. PIZZA PUFFS
24. MAC & CHEESE PIZZA
25. TACO PIZZAS
26. PIZZA CHILI
27. PIZZA NACHOS
28. PIZZA CRESCENTS
29. PIZZA CAULIFLOWER BAKE
30. PIZZA WAFFLES
31. PIZZA SLIDERS
32. PIZZA HOT DOGS
33. BEEF TACO SALAD PIZZA
34. PIZZA ROSES
35. FULLY LOADED STROMBOLI
36. PIZZA TORNADOS
37. CHICKEN PIZZA BURGERS
38. PIZZA STUFFED ZUCCHINI
39. BBQ CHICKEN PIZZA SLIDERS
40. PIZZA PEPPERONI BITES
41. PIZZA GRILLED CHEESE
42. CHEESY NOODLE PIZZA
43. MINI PEPPER PIZZAS
44. PIZZA SLOPPY JOES
45. PIZZA MAC & CHEESE

46. PIZZA SEVEN LAYER DIP
47. PIZZA TOT MUFFINS
48. SAUSAGE PIZZA SLIDERS
49. PIZZA ROLLS
50. SPAGHETTI SQUASH PEPPERONI PIZZA BOATS
51. PIZZA DIPPERS
52. PIZZA PULL-APART BREAD
53. PEPPERONI PIZZA PINWHEELS
54. PIZZA MAC & CHEESE
55. PIZZA NOODLE CUPS
56. GARLIC BREAD PIZZA DIP
57. PIZZA CAULIFLOWER CASSEROLE
58. MINI BREAKFAST PIZZAS
59. PIZZA KNOTS
60. PIZZA SOUP
61. CAULIFLOWER PIZZA BITES
62. PIZZA GNOCCHI
63. PIZZA ZUCCHINI BOATS
64. GREEK PITA PIZZAS
65. PIZZAGNA
66. PIZZA PASTA SALAD
67. MARGHERITA PIZZA FRIES
68. CHEESY BREAKFAST PIZZA
69. PRETZEL CRUST PIZZA
70. PEPPERONI PIZZA QUESADILLAS
71. CLASSIC PEPPERONI PIZZA
72. PEAR, PROSCIUTTO, AND GORGONZOLA PIZZA
73. BEST HOMEMADE MARGHERITA PIZZA
74. BUFFALO CHICKEN PIZZA
75. HAWAIIAN BBQ CHICKEN PIZZA
76. WISCONSIN BEER CHEESE SAUCE BACON PIZZA
77. CHEESEBURGER PIZZA
78. PEPPERONI PIZZA POT PIE
79. PIZZA CAKE
80. APPLE CHEDDAR PIZZA WITH CARAMELIZED ONIONS & WALNUTS
81. GARLIC-RANCH CHICKEN PIZZA
82. CHICKEN ALFREDO PIZZA
83. PIZZA HOMEMADE "HOT POCKETS"
84. CHICKEN FAJITA PIZZA
85. EASY PIZZA CASSEROLE
86. SPINACH ARTICHOKE PIZZA
87. RANCH PIZZA WITH WHITE CHEDDAR AND PROSCIUTTO
88. PIZZA PULL-APART BREAD
89. MEXICAN PIZZA FOR JUNE DAIRY MONTH
90. BEET PESTO PIZZA WITH KALE AND GOAT CHEESE
91. COBB SALAD PIZZA
92. PIZZA WITH SWISS CHARD, SAUSAGE, AND MOZZARELLA
93. EASY DINNER IDEA: 10 MINUTE MAC AND CHEESE PIZZA
94. PHILLY CHEESESTEAK PIZZA

95. SUN-DRIED TOMATO AND ARUGULA PIZZA
96. THREE CHEESE PESTO SPINACH FLATBREAD PIZZA
97. PIZZA ROLL-UPS
98. MINI DEEP DISH PIZZAS
99. GREEK PIZZA
100. SWEET POTATO, BALSAMIC ONION AND SOPPRESSATA PIZZA
101. THREE CHEESE PEACH AND PROSCIUTTO PIZZA WITH BASIL AND HONEY BALSAMIC REDUCTION
102. WHOLE-WHEAT PIZZA WITH ONIONS AND BITTER GREENS
103. TURKISH GROUND-LAMB PIZZAS
104. HUMMUS AND GRILLED-ZUCCHINI PIZZAS

1. SLOW-COOKER PIZZA

YIELDS: 4

PREP TIME: 0 HOURS 10 MINS

TOTAL TIME: 3 HOURS 10 MINS

INGREDIENTS

- Cooking spray, for slow cooker
- 1 lb. pizza dough
- 1 c. pizza sauce

- 2 c. shredded mozzarella
- 1/2 c. freshly grated Parmesan
- 1/2 c. sliced pepperoni
- 1/2 tsp. Italian seasoning
- pinch of crushed red pepper flakes
- 1 tsp. Freshly chopped parsley, for garnish

DIRECTIONS

1. Spray bottom and sides of a large slow cooker with nonstick cooking spray.
2. Press pizza dough into bottom of slow cooker until it reaches all edges and bottom is completely covered. Spoon over pizza sauce and spread, leaving about 1" of dough around edges. Top with cheeses, pepperoni, and spices.
3. Cover slow cooker and cook on low until crust turns golden and cheese is melty, 3 to 4 hours.
4. Remove lid and let cool 5 minutes.
5. Using a spatula, remove pizza from crock pot. Garnish with parsley, then slice and serve.

2. PRIMAVERA SKILLET PIZZA

YIELDS: 2

PREP TIME: 0 HOURS 15 MINS

TOTAL TIME: 0 HOURS 45 MINS

INGREDIENTS

- 2 bell peppers, sliced
- 1/2 head broccoli, florets removed
- 1/4 small red onion, thinly sliced
- 1 c. cherry tomatoes
- extra-virgin olive oil
- kosher salt
- Freshly ground black pepper
- All-purpose flour, for dusting surface
- 1 lb. pizza dough, at room temperature
- 1 c. ricotta
- 1 c. shredded mozzarella

DIRECTIONS

1. Heat oven to 400°. On a large baking sheet, toss peppers, broccoli, onion, and cherry tomatoes with olive oil and season with salt and pepper.
2. Roast until tender and tomatoes are bursting, 18 to 20 minutes. Remove and increase oven temperature to 500°.
3. Meanwhile, brush an oven-proof skillet with olive oil.
4. On a floured work surface, use your hands to roll out dough until it's the circumference of your skillet. Transfer to skillet and brush dough all over with olive oil.
5. Leaving a 1/2" border for crust, dollop spoonfuls of ricotta on dough and sprinkle with mozzarella.
6. Top with roasted vegetables and drizzle with olive oil. Sprinkle crust with salt.
7. Bake until crust is crispy and cheese is melted, about 12 minutes.

3. ZUCCHINI PIZZA CRUST

YIELDS: 4 - 6

PREP TIME: 0 HOURS 15 MINS

TOTAL TIME: 0 HOURS 50 MINS

INGREDIENTS

- 3 medium zucchini, or about 4 cups grated zucchini
- 1 large egg
- 2 cloves garlic, minced
- 1/2 tsp. dried oregano
- 3 c. shredded mozzarella, divided
- 1/2 c. grated Parmesan
- 1/4 c. cornstarch
- kosher salt
- Freshly ground black pepper
- 1/4 c. pizza sauce
- 1/4 c. pepperoni
- Pinch red pepper flakes, for garnish
- Basil, for garnish

DIRECTIONS

1. Preheat oven to 425° and line a baking sheet with parchment. On a box grater or in a food processor, grate zucchini. Using cheesecloth or a dish towel, wring excess moisture out of zucchini.
2. Transfer zucchini to a large bowl with egg, garlic, oregano, 1 cup mozzarella, Parmesan, and cornstarch and season with salt and pepper. Stir until completely combined.
3. Transfer "dough" to prepared baking sheet and pat into a crust. Bake until golden and dried out, 25 minutes.
4. Spread pizza sauce over crust then top with remaining mozzarella and pepperoni. Bake until cheese is melted and crust is crispy, about 10 minutes more. Garnish with red pepper flakes and basil.

4. GRILLED PIZZA BREAD

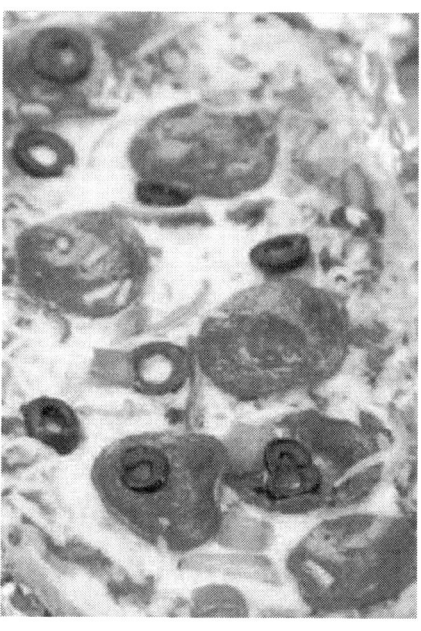

YIELDS: 6 - 8

PREP TIME: 0 HOURS 10 MINS

TOTAL TIME: 0 HOURS 25 MINS

INGREDIENTS

- 1 large loaf, halved
- 1 15-oz. jar pizza sauce
- 3 c. shredded mozzarella

- 1/3 c. pepperoni
- 1/4 c. black olives
- 1/2 red onion, cut into thin half moons
- 1 Green Bell Pepper, chopped
- pinch of crushed red pepper flakes

DIRECTIONS

1. Scoop out the middles from both bread halves to create shallow boats. Spread pizza sauce onto each half then top with mozzarella, pepperoni, black olives, red onion, green bell pepper, and red pepper flakes.
2. Wrap bread loosely with aluminum foil and place over campfire (or on a hot grill) and cook until the cheese is melty and the crust is toasted, 10 to 15 minutes.
3. Let cool for about 10 minutes until slicing. Serve warm.

5. BBQ CHICKEN SKILLET PIZZA

YIELDS: 2

PREP TIME: 0 HOURS 20 MINS

TOTAL TIME: 0 HOURS 45 MINS

INGREDIENTS

- 1 tbsp. extra-virgin olive oil, plus more for brushing
- 1/2 lb. boneless skinless chicken breasts, cut into cubes

- kosher salt
- Freshly ground black pepper
- Flour, for rolling out dough
- 1 lb. pizza dough, at room temperature
- 2 tbsp. barbecue sauce, plus more for drizzling
- 1/2 c. shredded cheddar
- 1/2 c. shredded fontina
- 1/4 small red onion, thinly sliced
- Ranch dressing, for drizzling
- Freshly chopped chives, for garnish

DIRECTIONS

1. Heat oven to 525°. In a large skillet over medium-high heat, heat oil. Add chicken and season generously with salt and pepper. Cook until golden and no longer pink, 8 minutes per side. Let rest 10 minutes, then slice into strips.
2. Meanwhile, brush an oven-proof skillet with olive oil. On a floured work surface, use your hands to roll out dough until it's the circumference of your skillet. Transfer to skillet.
3. Leaving a 1/2" border for crust, add barbecue sauce in a thin layer to dough. Top with cheddar, fontina, chicken and red onion. Brush crust with olive oil and sprinkle with salt. Bake until crust is crispy and cheese is melted, 23 to 25 minutes.
4. Drizzle with more barbecue sauce and ranch, garnish with chives, and serve.

6. LOW-CARB BREAKFAST PIZZA

YIELDS: 1

PREP TIME: 0 HOURS 5 MINS

TOTAL TIME: 0 HOURS 30 MINS

INGREDIENTS

- 4 large eggs
- 2 1/2 c. shredded mozzarella, divided
- 1/4 grated Parmesan, plus more for garnish
- kosher salt
- Freshly ground black pepper
- 1/4 tsp. dried oregano
- pinch red pepper flakes (optional)
- 2 tbsp. pizza sauce (or marinara)
- 1/4 c. mini pepperoni
- 1/2 Green Bell Pepper, chopped

DIRECTIONS

1. Preheat oven to 400° and line a baking sheet with parchment paper. In a medium bowl, combine eggs, 2 cups mozzarella, and parmesan. Stir until combined, then season with salt, pepper, oregano and red pepper flakes. Spread mixture into a ½" thick round on baking sheet.
2. Bake until lightly golden, about 12 minutes.
3. Spread pizza sauce on top of baked crust. Top with remaining mozzarella, pepperoni, and bell pepper.
4. Bake until cheese is melted and crust is crispy, about 10 minutes more. Sprinkle with Parmesan, if using, before serving.

7. MICKEY PIZZAS

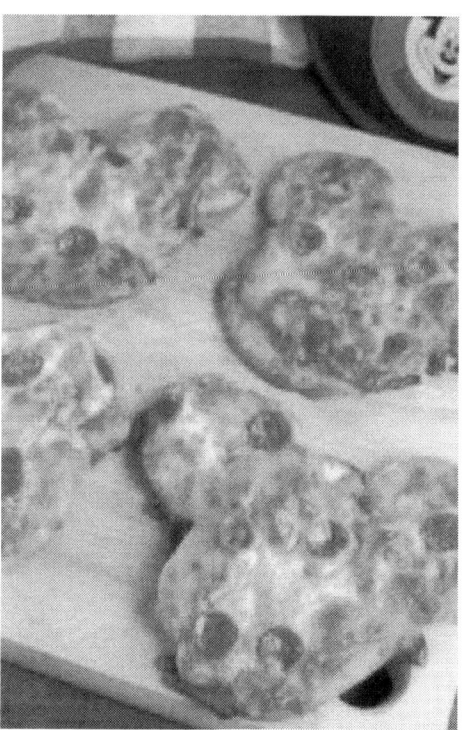

YIELDS: 8

PREP TIME: 0 HOURS 10 MINS

TOTAL TIME: 0 HOURS 25 MINS

INGREDIENTS

- Flour, for rolling out dough
- 1 sheet refrigerated pizza dough (preferably "Pillsbury")
- 1 can pizza sauce

- 2 c. mozzarella cheese
- 1 c. mini pepperoni
- 1/2 c. grated Parmesan
- 1 tsp. Italian seasoning

DIRECTIONS

1. Preheat oven to 375° and line two large baking sheets with parchment paper. On a lightly floured surface, unroll pizza dough. Using a 4" biscuit cutter, stamp out 8 circles, then use a 2" cookie cutter to cut out twice as many small rounds.
2. Divide the larger circles between the two prepared baking sheets. To each large round, place two smaller rounds on top to make the ears and pinch the pieces of dough together to seal. Spread pizza sauce onto each mickey dough. Top with mozzarella and pepperoni and sprinkle with Parmesan and Italian seasoning.
3. Bake until the cheese is melty and the crust is golden, 10 to 13 minutes. Serve warm.

8. EGG-IN-A-HOLE PIZZA BAGELS

YIELDS: 4

PREP TIME: 0 HOURS 15 MINS

TOTAL TIME: 0 HOURS 15 MINS

INGREDIENTS

- 2 tbsp. butter, divided

- 2 bagels, halved
- 1/2 c. pizza sauce
- 2 c. shredded mozzarella
- 1/3 c. mini pepperoni
- 2 tbsp. chopped fresh parsley
- 4 large eggs
- kosher salt
- Freshly ground black pepper
- Fresh basil, for garnish

DIRECTIONS

1. Melt 1 tablespoon butter in a nonstick skillet over medium heat. When the butter has melted, place the bagel halves in the skillet cut-sides down. Toast until golden.
2. Turn off the heat and place the bagel halves on a plate, toasted sides up. Use a cookie cutter (or small glass) to cut a bigger hole in the center of the bagel. Spread with pizza sauce and top with mozzarella and mini pepperoni. (Eat the buttery bagel scraps.)
3. Wipe the skillet clean with a paper towel. Melt remaining butter over medium heat and return the bagel to the skillet, pizza-side up. Crack an egg in the center of each hole and season the egg with salt and pepper to taste.
4. Cover the skillet with a large lid and cook until the cheese has melted and the egg has reached desired doneness, about 4 minutes for a runny sunny-side up egg.
5. Transfer to a serving plate and garnish with basil. Enjoy immediately.

9. CRUSTLESS PEPPERONI PIZZA

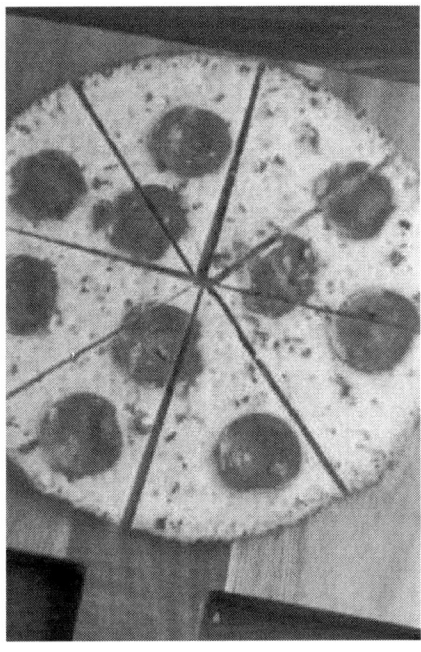

YIELDS: 1

PREP TIME: 0 HOURS 5 MINS

TOTAL TIME: 0 HOURS 15 MINS

INGREDIENTS

- 1 3/4 c. shredded mozzarella
- 1/4 c. freshly grated Parmesan
- 10 slices pepperoni
- 1/2 tsp. oregano
- pinch red pepper flakes
- 1 tsp. chopped parsley
- 1/2 c. marinara, heated, for dipping (optional)

DIRECTIONS

1. In an 8" non-stick skillet over medium heat, add mozzarella in an even layer. Top with parmesan and pepperoni. Cover with a glass lid and cook until cheese is completely melted and edges are golden. Top with oregano and red pepper flakes and remove from heat.
2. Let cool 3 minutes before sliding onto plate.

3. Garnish with parsley and slice. Serve with marinara for dipping if using.

10. PICKLE PIZZA

YIELDS: 4 - 6

PREP TIME: 0 HOURS 10 MINS

TOTAL TIME: 0 HOURS 30 MINS

INGREDIENTS

- 1 pre-made pizza crust
- 2 tbsp. olive oil
- 1 tsp. garlic powder
- 1 tsp. Italian seasoning
- 1 1/2 c. mozzarella
- 1/4 c. freshly grated Parmesan
- 1/2 c. sliced pickles, chopped
- 1 tbsp. fresh dill, chopped
- 1/2 tsp. red pepper flakes
- Ranch, for serving, if desired

DIRECTIONS

1. Preheat oven to 375 and line a large baking sheet with parchment paper.
2. In a medium bowl, combine olive oil with garlic powder and Italian seasoning. Place pizza crust on prepared baking sheet and brush all over with olive oil mixture.
3. Top crust with mozzarella and Parmesan and bake until cheese is melty, about 15 minutes. Remove from oven and add pickle slices to the top of the pizza and bake 5 minutes more.
4. Remove from oven and garnish with dill, more Parmesan, and red pepper flakes, if desired.
5. Slice and serve.

11. CAPTAIN AMERICA PIZZA

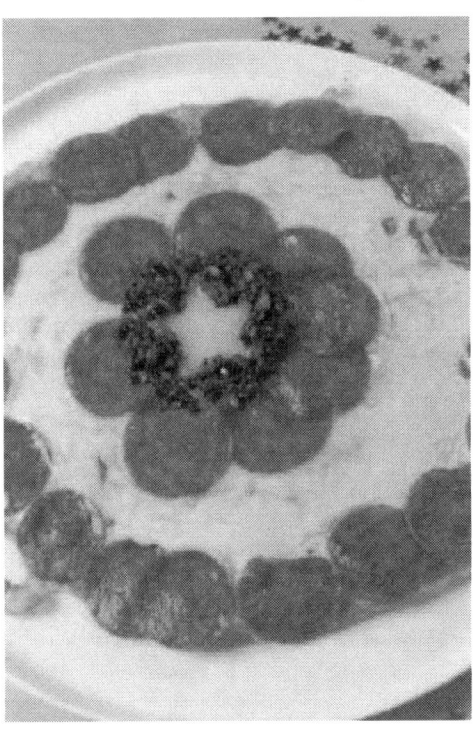

YIELDS: 6 - 8

PREP TIME: 0 HOURS 15 MINS

TOTAL TIME: 0 HOURS 30 MINS

INGREDIENTS

- 1 c. pizza sauce
- 4 large flour tortillas
- 3 c. shredded mozzarella
- 2 c. pepperoni

- 2 slices mozzarella
- 1 c. chopped black olives

DIRECTIONS

1. Preheat oven to 350° and line a large baking sheet with parchment paper. Working on the baking sheet, spread a thin layer of pizza sauce onto two tortillas then top each with a thin layer of shredded mozzarella and pepperoni.
2. Place the remaining two tortillas on top. Spread another layer of pizza sauce onto each quesadilla then cover each entirely with mozzarella.
3. Make a large ring of pepperoni, overlapping the slices, around the quesadilla, then make a smaller ring of pepperoni inside.
4. Using a star cookie cutter, arrange black olives in a star shape.
5. Bake for 15 minutes, or until cheese is melted.

12. CAULIFLOWER CRUST PIZZA

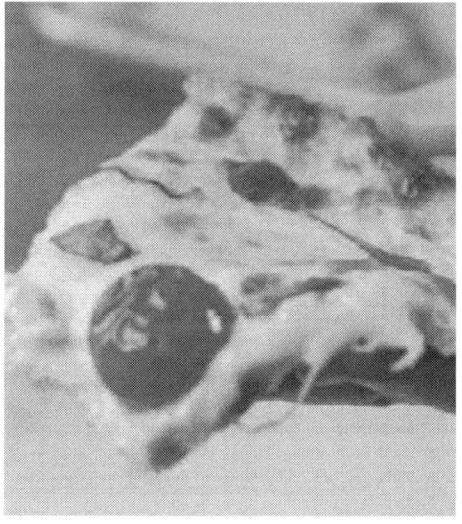

YIELDS: 4

PREP TIME: 0 HOURS 15 MINS

TOTAL TIME: 0 HOURS 45 MINS

INGREDIENTS

- 1 large head cauliflower, roughly chopped and steamed
- 1 large egg

- 2 c. shredded mozzarella, divided
- 1/2 c. freshly grated Parmesan, divided
- Zest from 1/2 lemon
- kosher salt
- Freshly ground black pepper
- 1/4 c. "RAGÚ Classic Alfredo Sauce"
- 1 clove garlic, thinly sliced
- 1/4 c. red onion, thinly sliced
- 1/4 c. cherry tomatoes, halved
- 1 small zucchini, shaved into a few lengthwise ribbons
- Torn fresh basil, for garnish

DIRECTIONS

1. Preheat oven to 425°. In a food processor, pulse steamed cauliflower until grated. Using a dish towel, squeeze out as much water as possible.
2. Transfer cauliflower to a large bowl and add egg, 1 cup mozzarella, 1/4 cup Parmesan and lemon zest. Season with salt and pepper.
3. Transfer dough to a parchment-lined, greased baking sheet and shape into a thin, round crust. Bake until golden and dried out, 20 minutes.
4. Top with "RAGÚ Classic Alfredo Sauce", remaining cheeses, garlic and vegetables and bake until cheese is melted and crust is crispy, about 10 minutes more. Garnish with basil.

13. THE WORKS SKILLET PIZZA

YIELDS: 2

PREP TIME: 0 HOURS 15 MINS

TOTAL TIME: 0 HOURS 40 MINS

INGREDIENTS

- 1 tsp. extra-virgin olive oil, plus more for brushing
- 2 Italian sausage links, casings removed
- All-purpose flour, for work surface
- 1 lb. pizza dough, at room temperature
- 1/4 c. pizza sauce
- 1 c. shredded mozzarella
- 1/4 c. sliced pepperoni
- 1 green bell pepper, sliced
- 1/4 small red onion, thinly sliced
- 1/4 c. sliced mushrooms
- 2 tbsp. sliced black olives
- kosher salt
- Freshly ground black pepper

DIRECTIONS

1. Heat oven to 525°. In a large skillet over medium heat, heat oil. Add sausage and cook, breaking up with the back of a wooden spoon, until golden and no longer pink, about 5 minutes.
2. Meanwhile, brush an oven-proof skillet with olive oil.
3. On a floured work surface, use your hands to roll out dough until it's the circumference of your skillet, then transfer to skillet.
4. Leaving a 1/2" border for crust, add pizza sauce in a thin layer to dough. Top with mozzarella, cooked sausage, pepperoni, green peppers, onion, mushrooms and olives, then season with salt and pepper.
5. Brush crust with olive oil and sprinkle with salt.
6. Bake until crust is crispy and cheese is melted, 23 to 25 minutes.

14. HAM, EGG, & CHEESE BREAKFAST PIZZA

YIELDS: 4

PREP TIME: 0 HOURS 10 MINS

TOTAL TIME: 0 HOURS 25 MINS

INGREDIENTS

- 1 lb. store-bought pizza dough, thawed if frozen
- 1 tbsp. extra-virgin olive oil, plus more for greasing pan
- 2 c. shredded mozzarella
- 1 c. diced ham
- 5 large eggs
- Freshly ground black pepper
- Fresh parsley, for garnish

DIRECTIONS

1. Preheat oven to 425°. Roll out pizza dough on a lightly greased pizza pan. Spread olive oil on top, then sprinkle evenly with mozzarella and ham. Crack eggs on top and sprinkle with pepper.
2. Bake until crust is golden brown and eggs are set, but still slightly soft, 15 minutes. Remove from the oven and slice warm. Garnish with parsley and serve.

15. CAULIFLOWER BREAKFAST PIZZA

YIELDS: 4

PREP TIME: 0 HOURS 25 MINS

TOTAL TIME: 0 HOURS 55 MINS

INGREDIENTS

- 1 large head cauliflower
- 8 large eggs, divided
- 1 c. shredded white Cheddar
- 2 cloves garlic, minced
- 1 tsp. paprika
- kosher salt
- Freshly ground black pepper
- 1 tbsp. extra-virgin olive oil
- 1 large onion
- 2 red bell peppers, chopped
- 1 c. ham
- 1 1/2 c. Shredded Monterey Jack
- Freshly chopped chives, for garnish

DIRECTIONS

1. Preheat oven to 425° and line a baking sheet with parchment. Grate cauliflower on small side of box grater to form fine crumbs. Transfer to a large bowl.
2. To bowl add 2 eggs, white cheddar, garlic, and paprika and season with salt and pepper. Stir until combined.
3. Transfer dough to prepared baking sheet and pat into a crust. Bake until golden and dried out, 25 minutes.
4. Meanwhile, in a large skillet over medium heat, heat oil. Add onion and peppers and cook until soft, 8 minutes. Stir in ham. In a small bowl, whisk together remaining 6 eggs and season with salt and pepper. Pour eggs into skillet and scramble, 3 minutes.
5. Remove cauliflower crust from oven and heat broiler. Spread a thin layer of salsa on top. Top with scrambled eggs and Monterey jack.
6. Broil until cheese is golden, 2 minutes.
7. Garnish with chives and serve.

16. SAUSAGE CAULIFLOWER PIZZA

YIELDS: 4

PREP TIME: 0 HOURS 20 MINS

TOTAL TIME: 0 HOURS 45 MINS

INGREDIENTS

- 1 large head of cauliflower or 2 small heads, cut into florets
- 1 1/2 c. freshly grated Parmesan
- 1 large egg
- 1 tbsp. extra-virgin olive oil
- kosher salt
- Freshly ground black pepper
- 1/4 c. marinara
- 1 tsp. chopped fresh oregano, plus more for garnish
- 8 oz. fresh mozzarella, drained and torn roughly into pieces
- 2 links Kielbasa sausage, thinly sliced

DIRECTIONS

1. Place pizza stone on middle rack and preheat oven to 500°. Line a sheet pan with parchment paper and set aside.
2. Fill blender halfway with water and add about half of the cauliflower florets. Pulse until cauliflower is size of rice granules. Drain into a colander and repeat with remaining cauliflower. If there are large pieces left pull them out and repeat process. Place cauliflower into a large bowl, cover with a paper towel and microwave for 5 minutes. Spread the cauliflower out on a sheet pan to speed up the cooling time. Squeeze out excess water using a cheesecloth or clean kitchen towel.
3. In a large bowl, combine cauliflower, Parmesan, egg, and oil and season with salt and pepper. Spread out evenly over parchment paper. Place sheet pan directly on pizza stone and bake for 10 minutes.
4. Meanwhile, in a large skillet over medium-high heat, sear sausage on one side for 3 to 4 minutes, then stir fry 1 more minute.
5. Spread marinara over cauliflower crust, leaving a 1-inch border. Sprinkle oregano all over and cover with pieces of mozzarella. Top with sausage and drippings from the pan. Bake 10 minutes and serve immediately with additional oregano.

17. CORNBREAD BREAKFAST PIZZA

YIELDS: 1

COOK TIME: 0 HOURS 35 MINS

TOTAL TIME: 0 HOURS 45 MINS

INGREDIENTS

- 1 box "JIFFY corn muffin mix"
- 1 egg
- 1/2 c. sour cream
- 1 c. shredded Cheddar cheese
- 6 slices bacon, cut into 1" pieces
- 6 eggs
- kosher salt
- Freshly ground pepper
- 2 green onions, sliced

DIRECTIONS

1. Preheat oven to 400 degrees F. Grease a 12" ovenproof skillet with cooking spray or olive oil.
2. Combine corn muffin mix, egg and sour cream in a large mixing bowl. Stir until smooth. Pour batter into the greased skillet and bake for 15-20 minutes, until golden.
3. Meanwhile, cook bacon in a nonstick skillet over medium heat until crispy. Turn off heat and transfer bacon to a paper-towel lined plate to drain fat.

4. Top the baked cornbread with cheese then crack the eggs on top. Scatter with bacon pieces and sprinkle eggs with salt and pepper.
5. Bake until egg whites are set but yolks are runny, 15 minutes. (If you prefer a less runny yolk, bake 18 to 20 minutes.)
6. Garnish with green onions, slice, and serve.

18. MINI DEEP-DISH PIZZAS

YIELDS: 12

PREP TIME: 0 HOURS 13 MINS

COOK TIME: 0 HOURS 12 MINS

TOTAL TIME: 0 HOURS 25 MINS

INGREDIENTS

- 4 (8-inch) flour tortillas
- 1 c. pizza sauce
- 3/4 c. shredded mozzarella cheese
- 1/4 c. freshly grated Parmesan cheese
- 48 slices mini pepperoni
- 2 tbsp. Freshly Chopped Basil

DIRECTIONS

1. Preheat the oven to 425°F. Lightly oil a 12-cup muffin tin, or coat it with nonstick spray.
2. Working one at a time, lay a tortilla on a flat surface. Using an empty 14 1/2-ounce can, cut out 3 rounds from the tortilla, pressing firmly and using a rocking motion to cut all the way through the tortilla. Repeat with the remaining tortillas.
3. Press a tortilla round into each of the 12 prepared muffin cups, pressing down carefully to create a well in the center of each cup. Scoop 1 tablespoon pizza sauce into each muffin tin. Sprinkle with the mozzarella and Parmesan, dividing it evenly, and top each pizza with 3 to 5 slices of mini pepperoni.
4. Bake for 10 to 12 minutes, or until both cheeses have melted.
5. Serve immediately, garnished with basil, if desired.

19. GLUTEN-FREE BROCCOLI CRUST PIZZA RECIPE

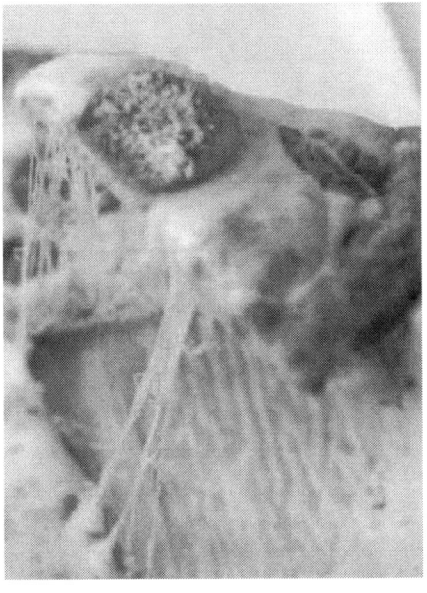

YIELDS: 4

PREP TIME: 0 HOURS 20 MINS

COOK TIME: 0 HOURS 30 MINS

TOTAL TIME: 0 HOURS 50 MINS

INGREDIENTS

- 1 large head broccoli, chopped and steamed
- 1 large egg

- 2 c. shredded mozzarella, divided
- 1/2 c. Parmesan, divided
- 1/2 tsp. garlic powder
- kosher salt
- Freshly ground black pepper
- 1/4 c. marinara sauce
- 1/4 c. pepperoni
- Fresh basil, for serving

DIRECTIONS

1. Preheat oven to 425 degrees F.
2. In a food processor, pulse steamed broccoli until grated. Squeeze water out in a dish towel. Transfer broccoli to a large bowl and add egg, 1 cup mozzarella, and ¼ cup Parmesan. Season with garlic powder, salt, and pepper.
3. Transfer dough to a parchment-lined, greased baking sheet and shape into a thin, round crust. Bake until golden and dried out, 20 minutes.
4. Top with marinara, remaining cheeses and pepperoni and bake until cheese is melted and crust is crispy, 10 minutes more. Garnish with basil.

20. DEEP DISH CAULIFLOWER PIZZA

YIELDS: 2

PREP TIME: 0 HOURS 15 MINS

TOTAL TIME: 0 HOURS 45 MINS

INGREDIENTS

- 1 large head cauliflower, grated (about 3 cups), squeezed dry of excess liquid
- 2 1/2 c. shredded mozzarella, divided
- 2 large eggs
- 1 c. freshly grated Parmesan, divided
- 1 tsp. garlic powder
- kosher salt
- Freshly ground black pepper
- 2 tbsp. pizza sauce
- 1/3 c. mini pepperoni
- Torn fresh basil, for garnish

DIRECTIONS

1. Preheat oven to 425° and grease a cast-iron skillet with cooking spray. In a large bowl, combine cauliflower, 1 cup mozzarella, eggs, 1/2 cup Parmesan, and garlic powder and season with salt and pepper.
2. Press mixture into skillet, making sure to get up the sides, and bake until deeply golden and dry, 25 minutes.
3. Spoon a thin layer of pizza sauce over crust and sprinkle with remaining mozzarella and Parmesan. Top with mini pepperoni and bake 5 minutes more.
4. Sprinkle with basil, slice, and serve.

21. BBQ CHICKEN CRUST PIZZA

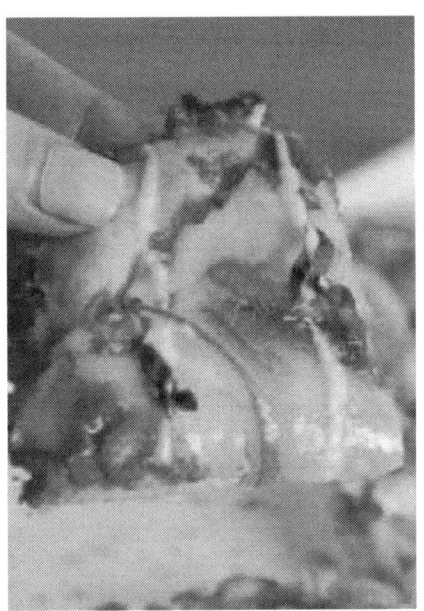

YIELDS: 4

PREP TIME: 0 HOURS 10 MINS

TOTAL TIME: 0 HOURS 35 MINS

INGREDIENTS

- 1 lb. ground chicken
- 1 1/2 c. shredded mozzarella
- 1 tsp. garlic powder
- kosher salt
- Freshly ground black pepper
- 1/4 c. barbecue sauce
- 1 c. shredded gouda
- 1/3 c. sliced red onion
- 2 tbsp. Sliced green onions
- Ranch, for drizzling

DIRECTIONS

1. Preheat oven to 400° and line a baking sheet with parchment. In a large bowl, stir together ground chicken, 1/2 cup mozzarella, and garlic powder and season with salt and pepper.
2. Spray prepared baking sheet and your hands with cooking spray. Form chicken mixture into pizza "crusts".
3. Bake until chicken is cooked through and golden, 20 to 22 minutes. Remove from oven and heat broiler.
4. Spread a thin layer of barbecue sauce on pizza crusts and top with remaining 1 cup mozzarella and gouda. Top with red and green onions and drizzle with more barbecue sauce.
5. Broil until cheese is melty, 3 minutes. Drizzle with ranch and serve.

22. PIZZADILLAS

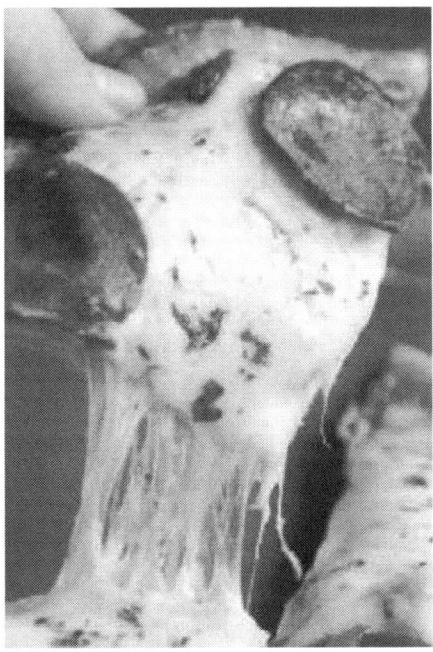

YIELDS: 1

TOTAL TIME: 0 HOURS 30 MINS

INGREDIENTS

- 1 tbsp. extra-virgin olive oil
- 2 medium flour tortillas
- 1/3 c. pizza sauce
- 1/3 c. pepperoni
- 1 c. shredded mozzarella
- 1/2 c. finely grated Parmesan
- 2 cloves garlic, minced
- Fresh italian parsley, chopped (for garnish)

DIRECTIONS

1. Heat olive oil in a medium ovenproof skillet over medium heat. Add one flour tortilla to the skillet and spread about half of the pizza sauce over the tortilla. Sprinkle with mozzarella and Parmesan.
2. Scatter garlic on top of the cheese and sprinkle Italian seasoning on top. Top with pepperoni, and top with the second tortilla. Cook until the cheese is melted and the tortilla is golden.

3. Meanwhile, preheat broiler. When ready to flip, cover the pan with a large plate. Invert pan to transfer the quesadilla onto the plate, then slide the quesadilla back onto the pan (golden side up). Top with remaining pizza sauce, mozzarella, Parmesan, Italian seasoning and pepperoni.
4. Place the skillet under the broiler and cook until the cheese is melted. Serve warm.

23. PIZZA PUFFS

YIELDS: 12

PREP TIME: 0 HOURS 15 MINS

TOTAL TIME: 0 HOURS 35 MINS

INGREDIENTS

- nonstick cooking spray
- 3 c. Bisquick
- 2 eggs
- 1 c. milk
- 3 tbsp. olive oil
- 2 tsp. Italian seasoning
- 3/4 tsp. kosher salt
- 1/2 tsp. garlic powder
- 3/4 c. mini pepperoni, plus more for garnish
- 1/2 c. grated Parmesan, plus more for garnish
- 8 mozzarella string cheese, cut into thirds
- Marinara (or pizza sauce), for dipping

DIRECTIONS

1. Preheat oven to 400°. Grease the bottoms of a 12-cup muffin tin with cooking spray. In a large bowl, combine Bisquick, eggs, milk, olive oil, salt, garlic powder and Italian seasoning. Whisk until just combined, then fold in mini pepperoni and Parmesan.
2. Scoop batter into muffin tin cups, then press a piece of string cheese into the center of each cup. Top with more pepperoni and bake until the muffins are golden and cooked through, about 20 minutes.
3. Sprinkle with Parmesan and serve warm with marinara.

24. MAC & CHEESE PIZZA

YIELDS: 4

PREP TIME: 0 HOURS 15 MINS

TOTAL TIME: 0 HOURS 40 MINS

INGREDIENTS

- 1 box macaroni and cheese, plus ingredients called for on box
- 1 c. shredded cheddar, divided
- 1 c. shredded mozzarella, divided
- 1 lb. pizza dough
- Extra-virgin olive oil, for brushing

- 1/4 tsp. garlic powder
- 1/4 tsp. Italian seasoning
- kosher salt
- Freshly ground black pepper
- Freshly chopped parsley, for serving

DIRECTIONS

1. Preheat oven to 450° and line a large baking sheet with parchment paper.
2. Prepare macaroni and cheese according to package instructions, then add ½ cup cheddar and ½ cup mozzarella to the pot. Stir until cheese is melted.
3. Stretch and roll pizza dough into a large round, about 12" wide. Transfer to the prepared baking sheet. Brush the top of the dough with olive oil and sprinkle with garlic powder. Bake until the crust begins to turn golden, about 10 minutes.
4. Spread the macaroni and cheese on top of the baked crust in an even layer, leaving a ½" border for the crust. Top with remaining cheddar and mozzarella and bake until the cheese is melted and the crust is golden, about 10 minutes more.
5. Garnish with parsley and serve warm.

25. TACO PIZZAS

YIELDS: 6

PREP TIME: 0 HOURS 10 MINS

TOTAL TIME: 0 HOURS 20 MINS

INGREDIENTS

- 1 tbsp. extra-virgin olive oil
- 1 medium onion, chopped
- 1 lb. ground beef
- 1 packet taco seasoning
- kosher salt
- Freshly ground black pepper
- 6 tostada shells
- 1 c. salsa
- 2 c. Mexican blend cheese
- 1 c. cherry tomatoes, cut into rounds
- 1 c. Shredded lettuce
- 1/2 c. sour cream
- Cilantro, for garnish

DIRECTIONS

1. In a medium skillet over medium heat, heat oil. Add onion and cook until tender, about 5 minutes. Add ground beef and taco seasoning, breaking up the meat with a wooden spoon. Season with salt and pepper, and cook until the beef is no longer pink, about 6 minutes. Drain fat and set aside.
2. Build your "pizza": spread a spoonful of salsa on your tostada shell, then top with cheese, meat, tomatoes, lettuce and a dollop of sour cream. Garnish with cilantro if desired and serve.

26. PIZZA CHILI

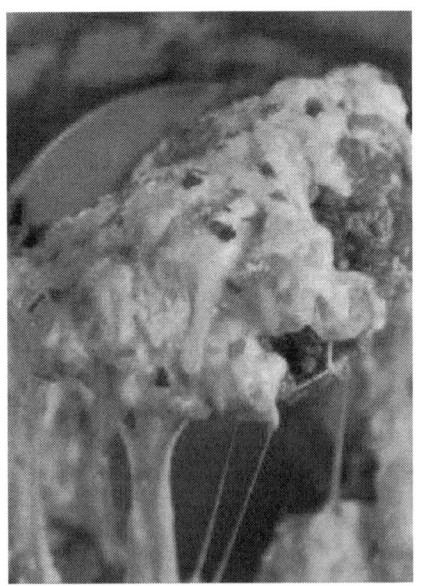

YIELDS: 6 - 8

PREP TIME: 0 HOURS 15 MINS

TOTAL TIME: 1 HOUR 0 MINS

INGREDIENTS

- 1 tbsp. olive oil
- 1/2 lb. spicy Italian sausage
- 1/2 lb. ground beef
- 1 yellow onion, chopped
- 1 Green Bell Pepper, chopped
- 1 c. sliced mushrooms
- 2 cloves garlic, minced
- 2 tsp. kosher salt
- 1 tsp. garlic powder
- 1 tsp. oregano
- 1/2 tsp. red chili flakes, plus more for garnish
- 2 c. chicken broth
- 2 c. pizza sauce
- 1 can fire roasted tomatoes
- 2 c. mozzarella
- 1/4 c. mini pepperoni
- 1 tbsp. chopped parsley
- 1/3 c. Parmesan

DIRECTIONS

1. In a large pot over medium heat, heat oil. Add sausage and beef and sauté until no longer pink. Remove from pot onto a paper towel lined plate. Drain fat if needed, reserving some for cooking vegetables.
2. Add onion, bell pepper, and mushrooms to the pot. Cook until onion is translucent and mushrooms and peppers have released some moisture, about 5 minutes. Add garlic and cook until fragrant, 1 minute. Season with salt, garlic powder, oregano, and chili flakes.
3. Add chicken broth, pizza sauce, and fire roasted tomatoes. Add back in the meat, stir, and bring to a simmer, stirring occasionally, for 25-30 minutes, until soup is thickened slightly.
4. Top pizza with mozzarella and pepperoni. Cover with a lid and let cheese melt, about 3 minutes.
5. Garnish with parsley, parmesan, and red chili flakes. Serve.

27. PIZZA NACHOS

YIELDS: 6 - 8

PREP TIME: 0 HOURS 10 MINS

TOTAL TIME: 0 HOURS 25 MINS

INGREDIENTS

- 1 bag Tortilla chips
- 2 c. pizza sauce
- 3 c. shredded mozzarella
- 1 Green Bell Pepper, chopped
- 1 c. mini pepperoni
- 1/2 c. sliced black olives
- 1/2 c. freshly grated Parmesan
- Chopped parsley, for garnish

DIRECTIONS

1. Preheat oven to 375°. Line a large baking sheet with foil.
2. On the prepared baking sheet, add about half of the chips. Drizzle about half the pizza sauce over the chips, then top with half of the mozzarella, half the pepperoni, bell pepper, black olives, and Parmesan . Repeat to make another layer with remaining ingredients.

3. Bake until the cheese is melted, about 15 minutes.
4. Garnish with parsley and serve immediately.

28. PIZZA CRESCENTS

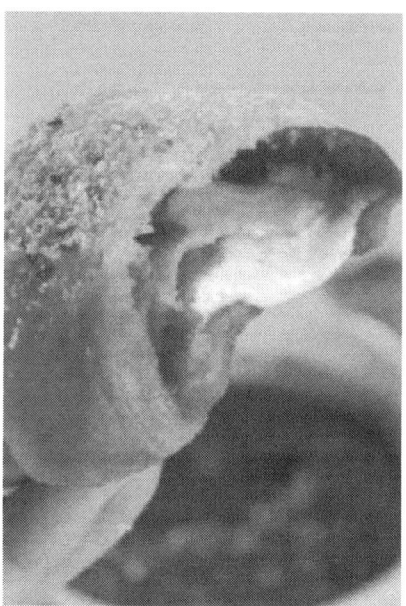

YIELDS: 4

PREP TIME: 0 HOURS 10 MINS

TOTAL TIME: 0 HOURS 25 MINS

INGREDIENTS

- 1 tube crescent roll dough
- 4 mozzarella sticks, halved
- 1/2 c. pepperoni
- 1 tbsp. olive oil
- 1/2 tsp. dried oregano
- 1/4 c. freshly grated Parmesan
- Marinara, for dunking

DIRECTIONS

1. Preheat oven to 350°. Line a large baking sheet with parchment paper.

2. Separate crescent dough into triangles. Top each triangle with an even layer of pepperoni then place a halved mozzarella stick on the wider end of the triangle and roll it up. Transfer crescents to the prepared baking sheet.
3. Brush each crescent with olive oil then sprinkle with oregano and Parmesan. Bake until the crescents are golden and the cheese has melted, about 15 minutes.
4. Serve warm with marinara for dunking.

29. PIZZA CAULIFLOWER BAKE

YIELDS: 6

PREP TIME: 0 HOURS 15 MINS

TOTAL TIME: 0 HOURS 45 MINS

INGREDIENTS

- 2 heads cauliflower, cut into florets
- 2/3 c. marinara
- kosher salt
- Freshly ground black pepper
- 2 c. shredded mozzarella, divided
- 2/3 c. freshly grated Parmesan, divided, plus more for garnish
- 1/2 c. sliced black olives
- 1/2 c. pepperoni, divided
- 1 tbsp. oregano, divided

- 2 tsp. crushed red pepper flakes, divided
- Fresh parsley, for garnish

DIRECTIONS

1. Preheat oven to 350°.
2. In a large bowl, combine cauliflower with marinara and toss until fully coated. Season with salt and pepper.
3. Place half the cauliflower in your baking dish, and top with half of the mozzarella, Parmesan, olives and pepperoni. Sprinkle with oregano and pepper flakes.
4. Add the rest of your cauliflower to the baking dish and repeat the topping process.
5. Bake until cauliflower is tender and cheese is bubbly, 30 minutes.
6. Let cool slightly, garnish with parsley and Parm and serve.

30. PIZZA WAFFLES

YIELDS: 1

PREP TIME: 0 HOURS 15 MINS

TOTAL TIME: 0 HOURS 15 MINS

INGREDIENTS

- Cooking spray, for waffle iron
- 2 cans refrigerated biscuits
- 3/4 c. shredded mozzarella, divided
- 1 tbsp. pizza sauce
- 1/2 c. mini pepperoni, divided
- Freshly grated Parmesan, for sprinkling
- Freshly chopped basil, for garnish

DIRECTIONS

1. Heat waffle iron and spray with cooking spray. Using your hands or a rolling pin, roll out biscuits into a flat patty. Top one biscuit with a layer of mozzarella, a spoonful of pizza sauce, and a layer of mini pepperoni. Sprinkle with Parmesan.
2. Top with remaining biscuit and seal edges. Top with another thin layer of sauce, mozzarella, and pepperoni. Place in waffle iron and cook until golden and cooked, about 3 minutes.
3. Garnish with basil and cut into 4 wedges.

31. PIZZA SLIDERS

YIELDS: 12

PREP TIME: 0 HOURS 25 MINS

TOTAL TIME: 0 HOURS 45 MINS

INGREDIENTS

- 12 slider buns, halved
- 1 tbsp. extra-virgin olive oil
- 1/2 onion, chopped
- 2 cloves garlic, minced
- 1 lb. ground beef
- 1 tsp. Italian seasoning, divided
- kosher salt
- Freshly ground black pepper
- pinch of crushed red pepper flakes
- 1 1/2 c. pizza sauce
- 12 slider rolls
- 2 c. shredded mozzarella
- 1/4 c. freshly grated Parmesan
- 2 tbsp. butter, melted
- 1 tsp. garlic powder
- 1/2 c. mini pepperoni

DIRECTIONS

1. Preheat oven to 350°. Place the bottom halves of the slider buns in a small sheet tray.
2. In a large skillet over medium heat, heat olive oil, add onion and cook until tender, 5 minutes. Stir in garlic and cook until fragrant, 1 minute more.
3. Add ground beef then season with 1/2 teaspoon of Italian seasoning, salt, and pepper. Cook, breaking up the meat with a wooden spoon, until the beef is no longer pink, about 6 minutes. Drain fat then add the pizza sauce. Let simmer for 5 minutes.
4. Spread ground beef mixture over the bottom buns, then sprinkle with about 1 cup mozzarella.
5. Place the top bun halves on top, then brush with melted butter and sprinkle with the remaining Italian seasoning and garlic powder. Sprinkle the remaining mozzarella and Parmesan on top then add the pepperoni. Bake until the cheese has melted and the buns are slightly toasted, about 10 minutes.
6. Let cool for 10 minutes in pan before serving.

32. PIZZA HOT DOGS

YIELDS: 6

PREP TIME: 0 HOURS 10 MINS

TOTAL TIME: 0 HOURS 20 MINS

INGREDIENTS

- 6 hot dog buns
- 1/4 c. butter, melted
- 1/2 tsp. garlic powder
- 6 hot dogs, boiled
- 1/2 c. pizza sauce
- 1 1/2 c. shredded mozzarella
- 1/2 tsp. Italian seasoning
- 1/2 c. mini pepperoni

DIRECTIONS

1. Preheat oven to 350°. Open hot dog buns and brush the inside with melted butter. Sprinkle with garlic powder. Place on baking sheet and bake until lightly golden, about 5 minutes.

2. Preheat broiler. Spoon a little sauce onto each hot dog bun then place boiled hot dog on top. Top each hot dog with mozzarella, sprinkle with Italian seasoning, then place mini pepperoni on top. Broil until the cheese is melty, about 2 minutes.

33. BEEF TACO SALAD PIZZA

YIELDS: 1

PREP TIME: 0 HOURS 10 MINS

TOTAL TIME: 0 HOURS 25 MINS

INGREDIENTS

- 1 1/2 tbsp. extra-virgin olive oil, divided
- 8 oz. lean ground beef
- 1 packet taco seasoning
- kosher salt
- Freshly ground black pepper
- 1 12" flour tortilla
- 1 1/2 c. shredded cheddar, divided
- 1 c. shredded romaine
- 1/4 c. sour cream
- 1 diced roma tomato
- 1/2 avocado, thinly sliced

DIRECTIONS

1. Preheat oven to 400°. Lightly grease a baking sheet with 1/2 tablespoon oil and set aside.
2. In a skillet, add remaining tablespoon oil and brown the beef, 3 to 4 minutes. Add taco seasoning and continue to brown until beef has cooked through, 4 to 5 minutes more. Lightly season with salt and pepper.
3. Place tortilla on greased baking sheet and top with 1/2 cup cheese. Top cheese with beef mixture and another 1/2 cup cheese. Bake until cheese has melted and tortilla has crisped up, 7 to 8 minutes.
4. Remove from oven and top with remaining cheese, shredded lettuce, sour cream, tomatoes, and avocado. Serve.

34. PIZZA ROSES

YIELDS: 12

PREP TIME: 0 HOURS 15 MINS

TOTAL TIME: 0 HOURS 40 MINS

INGREDIENTS

- 1 8-oz. tube crescent dough
- 1/4 c. pizza sauce
- 1 c. shredded mozzarella
- 1/2 c. freshly grated Parmesan

- 1 c. large pepperoni slices
- 1 tsp. Italian seasoning

DIRECTIONS

1. Preheat oven to 375° and spray a muffin tin with cooking spray.
2. On a lightly floured surface, unroll crescent dough and separate into 4 rectangles. If the dough has perforated edges, pinch together to seal.
3. Using a pizza cutter, cut each rectangle of dough lengthwise into three 1"-wide strips. Spread a very thin layer of sauce onto each strip. Sprinkle with cheeses, then layer pepperoni on top half of each strip so that they're slightly overlapping and the top halves of the pepperoni slices are off the pastry. Fold up bottom half of dough and tightly roll.
4. Transfer to prepared muffin tin and bake until golden, 15-20 minutes.
5. Serve warm.

35. FULLY LOADED STROMBOLI

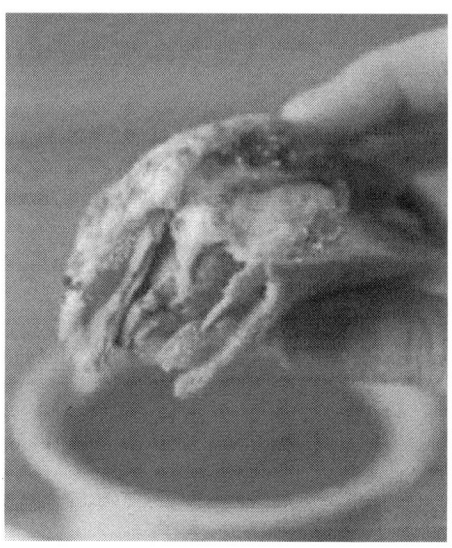

YIELDS: 4 - 6

PREP TIME: 0 HOURS 10 MINS

TOTAL TIME: 0 HOURS 35 MINS

INGREDIENTS

- 1 lb. pizza dough, at room temperature
- 1/2 c. "RAGÚ Old World Style Traditional Sauce"

- 4 slices ham
- 24 slices pepperoni
- 2 oz. cremini mushrooms, thinly sliced
- 1/2 Green Bell Pepper, chopped
- 1 c. shredded mozzarella
- 1 egg, beaten
- 1 tbsp. freshly grated Parmesan
- 1/2 tsp. Italian seasoning

DIRECTIONS

1. Preheat oven to 425°. Line a 12"-x-17" baking sheet with parchment paper. Stretch out dough into a large, thin rectangle and place on baking sheet. Spread with "RAGÚ Old World Style Traditional Sauce", leaving about an inch around the perimeter.
2. Top with ham, pepperoni, mushrooms, and peppers. Sprinkle with mozzarella then brush the perimeter with egg.
3. Gently roll up like a cinnamon roll, then pinch edges to seal and tuck under. Brush all over with egg, sprinkle with Parmesan and Italian seasoning, then make a few diagonal slits.
4. Bake until golden, 25 to 27 minutes. Let rest 5 to 10 minutes before slicing.

36. PIZZA TORNADOS

YIELDS: 4

PREP TIME: 0 HOURS 15 MINS

TOTAL TIME: 0 HOURS 35 MINS

INGREDIENTS

- 3 c. whole cherry or grape tomatoes
- 3 green bell peppers, cut into 1" pieces
- 2 c. small button mushrooms
- 1 1/2 c. sliced pepperoni
- 1/4 c. fresh basil leaves
- 1 tube refrigerated pizza dough
- 2 tbsp. extra-virgin olive oil
- 1 tbsp. Italian seasoning
- 1 c. shredded mozzarella
- Freshly ground black pepper

DIRECTIONS

1. Preheat oven to 400°. On 8 wooden skewers, thread cherry tomatoes, bell peppers, mushrooms, pepperoni, and basil.
2. On a large work surface, roll out pizza dough. Slice into thin ½" strips and wrap around skewered ingredients.
3. Brush skewers with olive oil, sprinkle with Italian seasoning, and season with pepper.
4. Bake until dough is deeply golden, 15 minutes, then remove from oven and sprinkle with mozzarella. Bake until melty, 5 minutes more.

37. CHICKEN PIZZA BURGERS

YIELDS: 4

PREP TIME: 0 HOURS 15 MINS

TOTAL TIME: 0 HOURS 30 MINS

INGREDIENTS

- 1 lb. ground chicken
- 2 cloves garlic, minced
- 1/4 c. chopped fresh parsley
- 1/4 tsp. crushed red pepper flakes
- kosher salt
- Freshly ground black pepper
- 2 tbsp. canola oil
- 4 slices mozzarella
- 16 slices pepperoni
- 1 c. "RAGÚ Homestyle Thick & Hearty Traditional Sauce"
- 4 Hamburger buns
- Torn fresh basil, for garnish

DIRECTIONS

1. In a medium bowl, combine ground chicken, garlic, parsley, and red pepper flakes. Season generously with salt and pepper and mix with spatula until just combined.
2. Using your hands, form 4 equally sized patties.
3. In a large skillet over medium heat, heat oil. Add the burgers and cook until golden and cooked through, 5 to 6 minutes per side.
4. Top each burger with a dollop of "RAGÚ Homestyle Thick & Hearty Traditional Sauce", a slice of cheese, and 4 slices pepperoni. Cover pan and let steam until cheese melts, about 2 minutes more.
5. In a small, microwave-safe bowl, heat remaining tomato sauce. Spread a dollop on each bottom bun followed by cooked burgers, basil, and top buns.

38. PIZZA STUFFED ZUCCHINI

YIELDS: 4

PREP TIME: 0 HOURS 15 MINS

TOTAL TIME: 0 HOURS 35 MINS

INGREDIENTS

- 4 medium zucchini
- 32 slices pepperoni, or more
- 8 slices mozzarella, or more, cut into eighths
- Italian seasoning
- 1/4 c. freshly grated Parmesan
- Marinara, warmed, for dipping

DIRECTIONS

1. Preheat oven to 425°.
2. Slice off both ends of zucchini and discard. Line up chopsticks on either side of zucchini, then carefully make 1/4" slices, making sure your knife hits the chopsticks. Repeat with remaining zucchini.
3. Place zucchini on a parchment-lined, rimmed baking sheet and bake until pliable, 10 minutes. Let cool until you can handle, then, alternating with pepperoni and mozzarella, stuff the slices of zucchini. Sprinkle each with a pinch of Italian seasoning and 1 tablespoon Parmesan. Bake until cheese is melty and pepperoni is crispy, 10 minutes more.

4. Serve with marinara for dipping.

39. BBQ CHICKEN PIZZA SLIDERS

YIELDS: 4 - 6

PREP TIME: 0 HOURS 20 MINS

TOTAL TIME: 0 HOURS 35 MINS

INGREDIENTS

- 12 Hawaiian rolls
- 3 c. shredded rotisserie chicken
- 1/2 c. barbecue sauce
- 1/4 c. diced red onion
- 1/4 c. freshly chopped cilantro
- 3 slices cheddar
- 1/4 c. butter
- 1 clove garlic, minced
- 1 tsp. onion powder

DIRECTIONS

1. Preheat oven to 350°. Slice slider rolls in half and place the bottom halves in a 9"-x-13" baking dish.
2. In a large bowl, add shredded chicken and barbecue sauce and stir to coat. Spoon chicken over the slider rolls and sprinkle with red onion and cilantro. Cut each slice of cheese into 4 pieces and top each slider with cheese. Place top of slider rolls over the sandwiches.
3. Place butter in a microwave-safe bowl and heat on low until melted, 30 seconds. Add garlic and onion powder and stir. Brush the tops of the sliders with garlic butter, then cover dish tightly with foil and bake, 15 minutes.

40. PIZZA PEPPERONI BITES

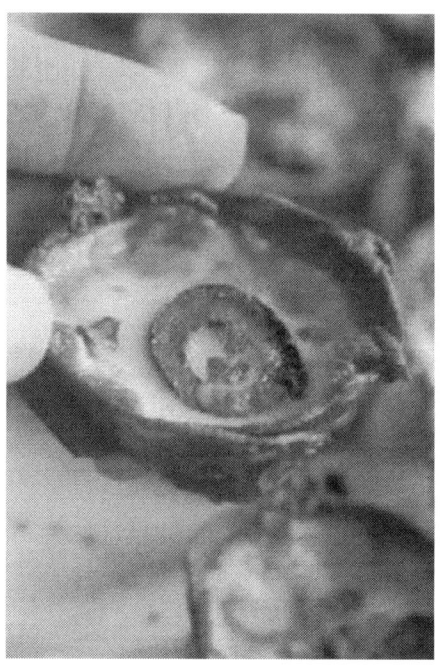

YIELDS: 1

PREP TIME: 0 HOURS 20 MINS

TOTAL TIME: 0 HOURS 20 MINS

INGREDIENTS

- 24 slices pepperoni
- 1 1/2 c. shredded mozzarella
- 1/4 c. pizza sauce
- 1/4 c. sliced black olives

- Chopped parsley, for garnish

DIRECTIONS

1. Preheat oven to 400°. On a cutting board, slice 4 slits in each slice of pepperoni so you can easily fold them over each other in the mini muffin tin. (Make sure to keep center intact.) Place a slice of epperoni in each muffin tin hole.
2. Bake until slightly crispy, 10 minutes. (If very greasy, remove pepperoni and blot with a paper towel. Blot pan with paper towel, then return pepperoni cups to pan.)
3. Heat broiler. Add a small spoonful of mozzarella, a small spoonful of pizza sauce, and another small spoonful mozzarella. Top with a couple black olives.
4. Broil until cheese is melty and golden, 2 minutes.
5. Garnish with chopped parsley and serve.

41. PIZZA GRILLED CHEESE

YIELDS: 1

PREP TIME: 0 HOURS 10 MINS

TOTAL TIME: 0 HOURS 20 MINS

INGREDIENTS

- 2 tbsp. butter
- 2 slices white or sourdough bread

- 1 tbsp. plus 2 tsp. pizza sauce
- 1 c. shredded mozzarella, divided
- 8 slices pepperoni, divided
- 1 tbsp. finely grated parmesan, plus more for garnish
- 1 fresh basil leaf
- Crushed red pepper flakes, for garnish

DIRECTIONS

1. Heat broiler. Assemble sandwich: Spread butter on the outside of two slices of bread. On the inside of one slice, spread 1 tablespoon pizza sauce, then top with 3/4 cup mozzarella, five slices of pepperoni, Parmesan, and basil. Top with remaining slice of bread, buttered side up.
2. In a large, oven-safe skillet over medium heat, cook sandwich until crispy, 5 minutes per side.
3. Spread remaining 2 teaspoons pizza sauce on top of sandwich, then top with remaining 1/4 cup mozzarella and remaining three pepperoni slices. Broil until cheese is melty and golden and pepperoni is crispy, 2 minutes.
4. Garnish with red pepper flakes and serve.

42. CHEESY NOODLE PIZZA

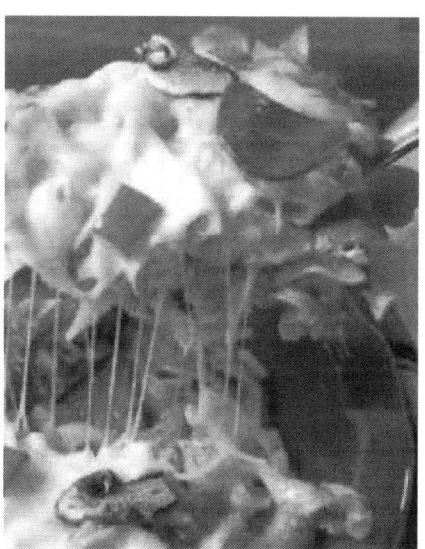

YIELDS: 6 - 8 SERVINGS

PREP TIME: 0 HOURS 15 MINS

COOK TIME: 0 HOURS 40 MINS

TOTAL TIME: 0 HOURS 55 MINS

INGREDIENTS

- 8 oz. "No Yolks® Extra Broad Noodles"
- 2 tbsp. extra-virgin olive oil
- 1 green bell pepper, chopped, some reserved for topping
- 1/2 pt. (4-oz.) sliced cremini mushrooms, some reserved for topping
- 2 cloves garlic, thinly sliced
- 1/3 c. pepperoni, some reserved for topping
- 1 c. marinara (or pizza sauce)
- kosher salt
- Freshly ground black pepper
- 1/4 tsp. crushed red pepper
- 2 c. shredded mozzarella, divided
- 1/2 c. parmesan, grated
- 6 large egg whites, beaten (or 3 large eggs)

DIRECTIONS

1. Cook "No Yolks Extra Broad Noodles" according to package directions. Drain and return to pot.
2. Preheat oven to 375 degrees F and grease a 9" pie dish. In a large skillet over medium heat, heat olive oil. Cook peppers and mushrooms until slightly softened, 6-8 minutes. Add garlic and cook until fragrant, 2 minutes more.
3. Turn off heat and stir in pepperoni and marinara. Season with salt, pepper, and crushed red pepper.
4. To pot of drained, cooked noodles, add marinara mixture, 1 cup mozzarella, and all of the Parmesan. Toss to coat. Transfer to prepared pie dish.
5. Pour over beaten egg whites and gently toss to incorporate. Sprinkle top with remaining mozzarella and garnish with extra pepperoni, mushrooms, and peppers.
6. Bake until set, 30 minutes. If desired, broil the top until golden, 2-3 minutes more. Let cool 15 minutes, then slice and serve.

43. MINI PEPPER PIZZAS

YIELDS: 4

TOTAL TIME: 0 HOURS 30 MINS

INGREDIENTS

- 4 bell peppers, halved and cored
- 1 tbsp. extra-virgin olive oil
- kosher salt
- Freshly ground black pepper
- 1/2 c. pizza sauce
- 2 c. shredded mozzarella
- 1/2 c. finely grated Parmesan
- 1/3 c. mini pepperoni
- 1 tbsp. chopped parsley

DIRECTIONS

1. Preheat oven to 350°.
2. On a sheet tray, drizzle peppers with olive oil and season with salt and pepper. Spoon sauce onto each pepper half. Sprinkle with mozzarella and Parmesan and top with pepperoni. Bake for 10-15 minutes, until the peppers are crisp-tender and the cheese is melted.
3. Garnish with parsley.

44. PIZZA SLOPPY JOES

YIELDS: 6

TOTAL TIME: 0 HOURS 20 MINS

INGREDIENTS

- 1 tbsp. olive oil
- 1 onion, chopped
- 1 bell pepper, chopped
- 1/2 c. pepperoni chopped (plus more for topping)
- 2 garlic cloves, minced
- 1 lb. ground beef
- kosher salt
- Freshly ground black pepper
- 1 tsp. Italian seasoning
- 2 c. pizza sauce
- 6 oz. sliced mozzarella
- 6 ciabatta rolls, toasted

DIRECTIONS

1. Heat olive oil in a large skillet over medium heat. Add onion and peppers and cook until they start to soften, about 5 minutes. Stir in pepperoni and cook until it starts to crisps, then add garlic and cook until, about 1 minute more.
2. Add ground beef, breaking up the meat with a wooden spoon. Cook until browned all over and cooked through. Drain fat.
3. Season with salt and pepper and Italian seasoning. Pour in pizza sauce and simmer for 5-10 minutes, until the flavors have melded. Inside the skillet, top the beef mixture with cheese and more pepperoni. Cover with more pepperoni and cover with lid to melt, 2 minutes.
4. Divide mixture between the ciabatta rolls and serve warm.

45. PIZZA MAC & CHEESE

YIELDS: 6

PREP TIME: 0 HOURS 25 MINS

TOTAL TIME: 0 HOURS 40 MINS

INGREDIENTS

- 16 oz. macaroni or shells
- 3 tbsp. butter
- 3 cloves garlic, minced
- 3 tbsp. all-purpose flour

- 2 1/2 c. milk
- 1 1/3 c. shredded mozzarella
- 1/2 c. shredded fontina
- 1/2 c. grated Parmesan, plus more for garnish
- 1 c. chopped pepperoni, plus 15 whole slices for topping
- 3/4 c. pizza sauce
- 1 tbsp. dried oregano
- 1 tsp. crushed red pepper flakes
- kosher salt
- Freshly ground black pepper
- Freshly chopped basil, for garnish

DIRECTIONS

1. Preheat oven to 375°. In a large pot of salted boiling water, cook macaroni according to package directions until al dente. Drain.
2. Add butter to pot and melt over medium heat. Add garlic and cook until fragrant, 1 minute. Sprinkle with flour and cook until golden, 1 minute more. Add milk and bring to a simmer. Let thicken, 3 minutes. Add 1 cup mozzarella, fontina, and Parmesan and stir until melty, 2 minutes more.
3. Add cooked macaroni and stir until completely coated, then stir in chopped pepperoni, 1/2 cup pizza sauce, dried oregano, and crushed red pepper flakes. Season with salt and pepper.
4. Transfer mac to a baking dish and spoon remaining 1/4 cup pizza sauce on top. Top with remaining mozzarella and whole pepperoni.
5. Bake until cheese is melty and golden and pepperoni crispy, 15 minutes.
6. Garnish with basil and Parmesan and serve.

46. PIZZA SEVEN LAYER DIP

YIELDS: 8 - 10

PREP TIME: 0 HOURS 10 MINS

COOK TIME: 0 HOURS 5 MINS

TOTAL TIME: 0 HOURS 15 MINS

INGREDIENTS

- 2 c. ricotta
- 2 tbsp. chopped Italian parsley
- 1 c. marinara sauce, warmed
- 1 1/2 c. shredded Parmesan
- 1 c. chopped pepperoncini
- 1 1/2 c. sliced black olives
- 10 oz. low moisture mozzarella, sliced
- 1 c. mini pepperoni
- 1 tbsp. fresh basil, thinly sliced
- Toasted baguette slices

DIRECTIONS

1. Preheat broiler to medium. Grease a 9-x-9" dish baking dish with cooking spray.

2. Spread ricotta into an even layer on the bottom of the baking dish. Sprinkle parsley over the ricotta, then spread a thin layer of marinara over the herbs. Top with single layers each of Parmesan, pepperoncini, black olives, mozzarella and pepperoni. Broil until the cheese has melted.
3. Garnish with basil and serve warm with the baguette slices.

47. PIZZA TOT MUFFINS

YIELDS: 1

INGREDIENTS

- 1 c. marinara sauce
- 2 Eggs, beaten
- 1 1/2 c. shredded mozzarella cheese, divided
- 1/4 c. freshly grated Parmesan cheese
- 1/2 c. mini pepperoni, divided
- 1/2 tsp. dried oregano
- 1/2 tsp. garlic powder
- kosher salt
- Freshly ground black pepper
- 2 (16 oz.) bags "Green Giant Cauliflower Veggie Tots"

DIRECTIONS

1. Preheat the oven to 425 degrees F. Grease a 12-cup muffin tin.
2. In a large bowl, combine marinara sauce, eggs, 1 cup mozzarella, Parmesan, 1/4 cup pepperoni, oregano, and garlic powder. Season with salt and pepper.
3. Toss in tots and mix until evenly coated. Pack into muffin cups, then sprinkle with remaining mozzarella and pepperoni.

4. Bake until muffins are crispy and cheese is melty, 20 to 22 minutes. Cool slightly before removing.

48. SAUSAGE PIZZA SLIDERS

YIELDS: 4

PREP TIME: 0 HOURS 10 MINS

TOTAL TIME: 0 HOURS 25 MINS

INGREDIENTS

- Olive oil spray
- 9 Slider buns
- 4 sweet Italian sausage links
- 12 slices mozzarella
- 1 c. marinara
- 1 tbsp. salted butter, melted
- 2 tbsp. chopped fresh parsley, plus more for garnish
- 2 tbsp. freshly grated Parmesan, plus more for garnish

DIRECTIONS

1. Preheat oven 350°. Spray baking dish with olive oil spray and place bottom slider buns inside.

2. Spray a large skillet with olive oil spray. Heat over medium-high and brown sausage evenly until cooked through, about 5 minutes. Transfer to cutting board and rest for a few minutes before slicing into 1/4-inch diagonal pieces.
3. Place an even layer of mozzarella over buns, layer with sausage slices and a spoonful of marinara. Cover with an even layer of mozzarella and place slider tops on top. Brush with melted butter and top with sprinkle of parsley and Parmesan. Cover with foil and bake 10 minutes, then remove foil and bake until cheese is melted and tops are lightly golden, about 5 minutes.
4. Sprinkle with additional parsley and Parmesan. Serve warm.

49. PIZZA ROLLS

YIELDS: 10

PREP TIME: 0 HOURS 10 MINS

COOK TIME: 0 HOURS 15 MINS

TOTAL TIME: 0 HOURS 25 MINS

INGREDIENTS

- 1 tube refrigerated pizza dough
- 1 c. pizza or marinara sauce
- 1/2 c. mini pepperoni
- 1 tsp. dried oregano
- 2 c. shredded mozzarella
- 1/2 c. finely grated Parmesan

- 1 pinch red pepper flakes

DIRECTIONS

1. Preheat oven to 375 degrees F. Line a baking sheet with parchment paper and place in oven.
2. Roll pizza dough into a large rectangle, then cut dough crosswise into 4 smaller rectangles. Dust pizza dough with flour if needed. Spread a thin layer of pizza sauce over each rectangle, leaving 1" border along one long side. Sprinkle cheeses and oregano over each rectangle and top with pepperoni.
3. Roll up each rectangle, starting with one short side. Press the edges together to seal. Repeat with remaining dough. Cut each roll into 1" slices using a serrated knife.
4. Place on baking sheet. Bake 15-20 minutes or until edges are golden brown. Serve warm.

50. SPAGHETTI SQUASH PEPPERONI PIZZA BOATS

YIELDS: 4

PREP TIME: 0 HOURS 15 MINS

TOTAL TIME: 0 HOURS 55 MINS

INGREDIENTS

- 2 whole spaghetti squash
- kosher salt
- Freshly ground black pepper

- Extra-virgin olive oil, for drizzling
- 1 c. chopped pepperoni
- 2 c. marinara
- 2 c. shredded mozzarella
- 1/4 c. chopped parsley

DIRECTIONS

1. Preheat oven to 400°. Place spaghetti squash on a plate and microwave 5 minutes. Halve each lengthwise and remove any seeds (be careful of hot steam!). Transfer to a parchment-lined baking sheet, season with salt and pepper, and drizzle with olive oil.
2. Bake, cut-side down, for 30 minutes. Remove from oven and heat broiler.
3. Meanwhile, in a small skillet over medium heat, crisp pepperoni, stirring occasionally. Transfer to a plate.
4. Loosen spaghetti strands using a fork. Add 1/2 cup marinara, 1/4 cup mozzarella, and 1/4 cup crispy pepperoni to each baked squash half. Mix filling with a fork and top with 1/4 cup more mozzarella and parsley. Return to baking sheet.
5. Broil until cheese is melted and golden, 4 to 5 minutes. Serve immediately.

51. PIZZA DIPPERS

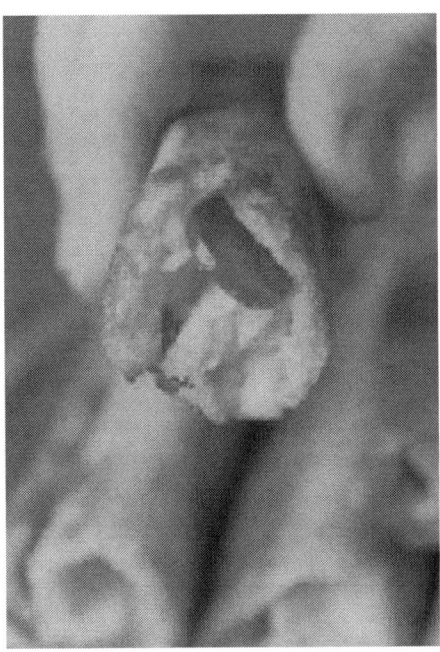

YIELDS: 8

TOTAL TIME: 0 HOURS 5 MINS

INGREDIENTS

- 8 slices white bread, crusts removed
- 1 c. shredded mozzarella
- 1/2 c. mini pepperoni
- 4 tbsp. butter
- Marinara sauce, warmed, for serving

DIRECTIONS

1. Using a rolling pin, roll bread into flat, ¼-inch thick squares. Add a large pinch of shredded cheese to bread, then sprinkle with 5-6 pepperoni. Roll up tightly.
2. Melt 1 tablespoon butter in a large nonstick skillet over medium heat. Working in batches, add the roll ups to the skillet, seam side-down. Cook, turning often, until all sides are golden and cheese has melted, about 3 minutes. Wipe the skillet clean and add more butter before adding more roll-ups.
3. Serve with warm marinara sauce.

52. PIZZA PULL-APART BREAD

YIELDS: 1

COOK TIME: 0 HOURS 30 MINS

TOTAL TIME: 0 HOURS 35 MINS

INGREDIENTS

- 1 roll Pillsbury pizza crust
- 1/4 c. pizza sauce
- 4 cloves garlic, minced
- 1 1/2 c. shredded mozzarella
- 1/2 c. grated Parmesan
- 1/2 c. sliced pepperoni
- 1/2 tsp. dried oregano

DIRECTIONS

1. Preheat oven to 400°. Roll out pizza crust on a floured work surface.
2. Spoon a thin layer of pizza sauce and top with garlic.
3. Trim sides so you have a clean square.
4. Sprinkle mozzarella and Parmesan all over the sauce.
5. Top with pepperoni.
6. Slice dough into squares and stack on top of each other.
7. Place sideways in a greased loaf pan.
8. Bake until pizza crust is cooked through, 30 minutes.
9. Turn out on a serving plate and serve.

53. PEPPERONI PIZZA PINWHEELS

YIELDS: 4

PREP TIME: 0 HOURS 10 MINS

TOTAL TIME: 0 HOURS 30 MINS

INGREDIENTS

- 1/4 c. marinara
- 1 tsp. dried oregano
- All-purpose flour, for rolling
- 1 Large ball pizza dough
- 8 oz. low-moisture mozzarella, sliced
- 8 oz. thinly sliced pepperoni

DIRECTIONS

1. Line a sheet pan with parchment paper and place in oven. Preheat oven to 500°.
2. Meanwhile, in a small bowl combine marinara and oregano. Set aside.
3. Lightly flour work surface. Stretch and roll pizza dough into a rectangle, dusting dough with flour if needed. Spread a thin layer of tomato sauce over dough, leaving a 1" border along one long side. In an even layer, repeat with an even layer of mozzarella. Tightly roll along the long edge into a jelly roll shape, then remove excess flour with a dry pastry brush. Transfer to sheet pan seam-side down.
4. Bake for 10 to 12 minutes. Let cool for 5 minutes, then cut into 1/2" slices. Serve immediately.

54. PIZZA MAC & CHEESE

YIELDS: 4

PREP TIME: 0 HOURS 15 MINS

TOTAL TIME: 0 HOURS 25 MINS

INGREDIENTS

- kosher salt
- 1 lb. penne
- 3 tbsp. unsalted butter
- 3 tbsp. all-purpose flour
- 1/4 c. tomato paste
- 2 c. whole milk
- 1 tsp. dried oregano, plus more for garnish
- 1/2 tsp. crushed red pepper flakes
- 3 c. grated mozzarella
- 1/4 lb. mini pepperoni slices

DIRECTIONS

1. Preheat oven 375°. In a large pot of salted boiling water, cook pasta according to package directions until al dente, less 2 minutes.
2. Meanwhile, in a large cast-iron skillet over medium-high heat, melt butter, whisk in flour, and cook for 1 minute. Add tomato paste and whisk in milk until smooth. Add oregano, red pepper flakes, and 1/2 teaspoon salt and bring to a boil. Simmer for 1 minute on medium heat.
3. Fold in half the cheese and add drained pasta. Top pasta with remaining cheese and sprinkle pepperoni all over.
4. Bake until pepperoni is crispy and pasta is bubbling, 10 minutes. Serve immediately.

55. PIZZA NOODLE CUPS

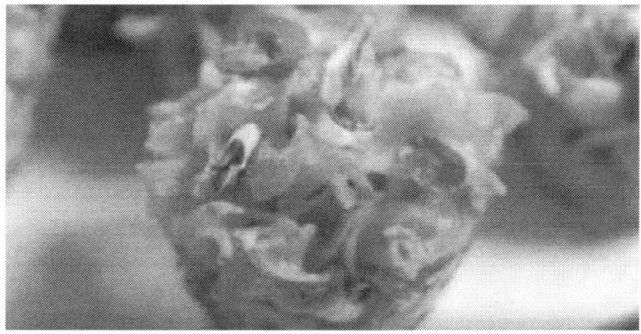

YIELDS: 1

INGREDIENTS

- Cooking spray, for muffin tin
- 12 oz. "No Yolks® Extra Broad Noodles"
- 2 large eggs, beaten (or 4 egg whites)
- 1/2 c. grated Parmesan
- 2 1/2 c. shredded mozzarella
- 1 c. marinara
- 4 oz. cream cheese, softened
- 2 cloves garlic, minced
- 1 tsp. dried oregano
- 1/2 tsp. crushed red pepper flakes
- kosher salt
- Freshly ground black pepper
- 1 c. mini pepperoni, divided

- Torn fresh basil, for garnish

DIRECTIONS

1. Preheat oven to 350F and grease a nonstick muffin tin with cooking spray. Cook noodles according to package directions. Drain.
2. In a small bowl, combine eggs, Parmesan, 2 cups mozzarella, marinara, cream cheese, garlic, oregano, and red pepper flakes. Season with salt and pepper, then add ½ cup pepperoni. Add cooked noodles and toss until fully combined.
3. Fill muffin cups with noodle mixture and sprinkle with remaining mini pepperoni. Season with salt and pepper.
4. Bake until cups are set and pepperoni are crisp, 30 minutes.
5. Garnish with basil.

56. GARLIC BREAD PIZZA DIP

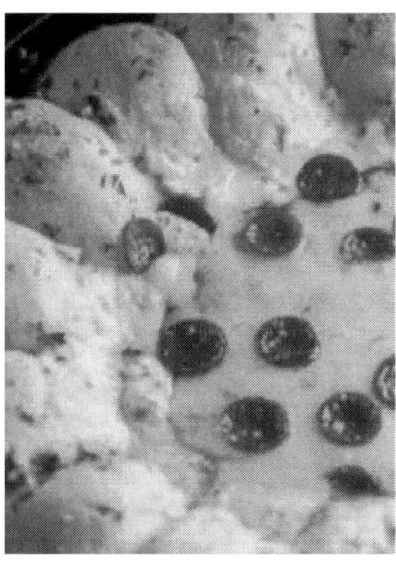

YIELDS: 8

PREP TIME: 0 HOURS 15 MINS

TOTAL TIME: 0 HOURS 55 MINS

INGREDIENTS

- 2 c. shredded mozzarella, divided

- 8 oz. cream cheese, softened
- 1/2 c. ricotta
- 1/4 c. plus 1 tbsp. freshly grated Parmesan, divided
- 1 tbsp. Italian seasoning
- 1/2 tsp. crushed red pepper flakes
- kosher salt
- 1 can refrigerated biscuits (such as Pillsbury Grands)
- 2 tbsp. extra-virgin olive oil
- 3 cloves garlic, minced
- 1 tbsp. Freshly Chopped Parsley
- 1/4 c. pizza sauce or marinara
- 1/4 c. mini pepperoni

DIRECTIONS

1. Preheat oven to 350°. Make dip: In a large bowl combine 1 1/4 cup mozzarella, cream cheese, ricotta, 1/4 cup Parmesan, Italian seasoning, and red pepper flakes and season with salt. Stir to combine.
2. Halve biscuits and roll into balls. Place in skillet in a ring. In a small bowl, combine olive oil, garlic, and parsley. Brush on biscuits.
3. Place dip inside of ring and spoon over marinara. Top with remaining 3/4 cup mozzarella and mini pepperoni. Sprinkle remaining tablespoon Parmesan all over.
4. Bake until biscuits are golden and cheese is melty, about 30 minutes. (Brush biscuits with more olive oil halfway through if necessary.)
5. Blot any grease from pepperoni (or don't!), let cool 10 minutes, then serve.

57. PIZZA CAULIFLOWER CASSEROLE

YIELDS: 1

PREP TIME: 0 HOURS 25 MINS

COOK TIME: 0 HOURS 30 MINS

TOTAL TIME: 0 HOURS 55 MINS

INGREDIENTS

- 2 heads of cauliflower, sliced
- 1 14.5-oz. can crushed tomatoes
- 1 c. ricotta
- 2 tbsp. extra-virgin olive oil
- 1 tsp. "McCormick Oregano Leaves"
- 1 tsp. "McCormick Garlic Powder"
- Pinch of "McCormick Crushed Red Pepper Salt"
- Pepper
- 2 c. Mozzarella, shredded
- 1/2 c. Parmesan, shredded
- 1 c. pepperoni, divided

DIRECTIONS

1. Preheat oven to 375 degrees F. Steam the cauliflower with water in a covered pot to desired tenderness, and set aside. In a saucepan, simmer crushed tomatoes with olive oil and spices. Stir in ricotta.
2. In a large bowl, mix cauliflower with sauce. In another bowl, mix together mozzarella and Parmesan.
3. In a large baking dish, layer ½ cauliflower mixture, and top with ½ cheese mixture. Top with ½ cup pepperoni. Repeat process a second time to fill dish.
4. Bake 25-30 minutes.

58. MINI BREAKFAST PIZZAS

YIELDS: 2

COOK TIME: 0 HOURS 10 MINS

TOTAL TIME: 0 HOURS 20 MINS

INGREDIENTS

- 2 english muffins, halved
- 1 tbsp. butter, plus 1 tablespoon melted butter (optional)
- 4 eggs
- 1 tbsp. milk
- kosher salt
- Freshly ground pepper
- 1/3 c. shredded cheese (see topping ideas below)

PIZZERIA-STYLE

- 1/4 c. mini pepperoni
- 1/3 c. shredded mozzarella
- 1 tbsp. finely chopped parsley

BEC-STYLE

- 2 slices of bacon, cooked and crumbled
- 1/3 c. sharp shredded Cheddar
- 1 tbsp. finely chopped chives

DIRECTIONS

1. Preheat oven to 350 degrees F. Grease a baking sheet with olive oil or cooking spray.
2. Whisk together eggs and cream in a medium bowl until light and frothy.
3. Melt butter in a medium nonstick skillet over medium-low heat then add the egg mixture. Stir occasionally with a spatula or wooden spoon. When the eggs are nearly set, season with salt and pepper and remove from heat.
4. Place English muffin halves, cut side up on the baking tray. Brush with melted butter, if desired. Sprinkle each piece with your cheese of choice then top with eggs then sprinkle with more cheese. Add desired toppings (see above).
5. Bake for 10 minutes, until the cheese is melted and the English muffin is slightly toasted. Garnish with fresh herbs.

59. PIZZA KNOTS

YIELDS: 8 - 10

PREP TIME: 0 HOURS 20 MINS

TOTAL TIME: 0 HOURS 40 MINS

INGREDIENTS

- 2 tbsp. melted butter
- 1/4 c. extra-virgin olive oil
- 2 cloves garlic, minced
- 2 tbsp. chopped parsley
- 1/2 c. finely grated Parmesan
- 1 can refrigerated biscuit dough
- 2/3 c. shredded mozzarella
- 1/2 c. mini pepperoni
- Marinara, warmed (for serving)

DIRECTIONS

1. Preheat oven to 400° and grease a 10" skillet with cooking spray or olive oil.
2. Whisk together butter, olive oil, garlic, parsley, and Parmesan.
3. Cut each biscuit in half and shape each half into a thin rectangle. Brush each piece with butter mixture, then sprinkle lightly with mozzarella and pepperoni. Roll and pinch the dough together to seal, then tie the dough into knots.
4. Place stuffed knots in the skillet. Brush remaining butter mixture onto dough and sprinkle with more mozzarella and pepperoni.
5. Bake until the cheese is melted and the biscuits are cooked through, 18 to 20 minutes. Serve warm with marinara.

60. PIZZA SOUP

YIELDS: 4

TOTAL TIME: 0 HOURS 35 MINS

INGREDIENTS

- 1 tbsp. extra-virgin olive oil
- 1 large onion, chopped
- 2 red and/or green bell peppers, chopped
- kosher salt
- 8 oz. sliced baby bella mushrooms
- 3 cloves garlic, minced
- 2 tbsp. tomato paste
- 1 c. chopped pepperoni, plus whole pepperoni slices for topping
- 1 tbsp. Italian seasoning
- 1 tsp. crushed red pepper flakes
- 28 oz. can crushed tomatoes
- 4 c. low-sodium chicken broth
- 1/2 c. heavy cream
- 1 crusty baguette, cut into 4"-long pieces
- 2 c. shredded mozzarella
- Chopped fresh parsley, for garnish

DIRECTIONS

1. In an ovenproof Dutch oven or soup pot over medium heat, heat oil. Add onions and peppers and season with salt. Cook until slightly tender and golden, 3 minutes, then add mushrooms and cook until browned and juices have evaporated, 8 minutes more. Add garlic and tomato paste and cook until fragrant, 1 minute. Add chopped pepperoni and stir until combined.
2. Add Italian seasoning, crushed red pepper flakes, crushed tomatoes, and chicken broth and bring to a simmer, 20 minutes.
3. Remove from heat and stir in heavy cream. Heat broiler.
4. Top pot with bread and sprinkle with mozzarella. Place remaining pepperoni on top and carefully transfer soup to oven until cheese is melty and golden.
5. Garnish with parsley and serve.

61. CAULIFLOWER PIZZA BITES

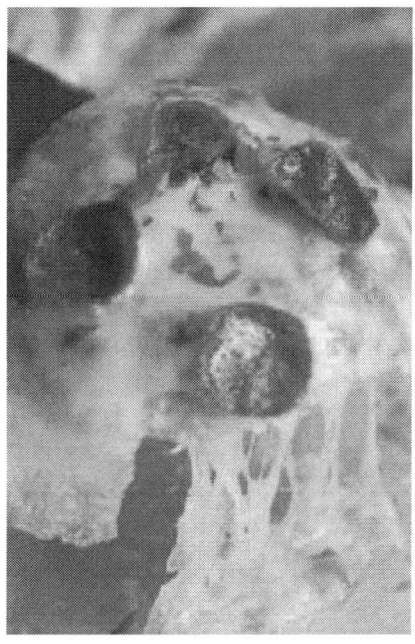

YIELDS: 6

PREP TIME: 0 HOURS 15 MINS

TOTAL TIME: 0 HOURS 45 MINS

INGREDIENTS

- 1 large head cauliflower
- 2 large eggs
- 1 c. shredded mozzarella, divided
- 1/4 c. freshly grated Parmesan
- 3 tbsp. finely chopped fresh basil, divided
- 1 tbsp. garlic powder
- kosher salt
- Freshly ground black pepper
- 1/2 c. marinara
- 1/4 c. mini pepperoni

DIRECTIONS

1. Preheat oven to 400°. Grate cauliflower on the small side of a box grater to form fine crumbs. Transfer to a large bowl.

2. Add eggs, 1/3 cup mozzarella, Parmesan, 2 tablespoons basil, and garlic powder to bowl and season with salt and pepper. Form into small patties (they will be wet) and place on a greased baking sheet. Bake until golden, 20 minutes.
3. Top each cauli patty with a thin layer of marinara, a sprinkle of the remaining mozz, and mini pepperoni and bake until cheese melts and pepperoni crisps, 5 to 7 minutes more.
4. Garnish with remaining basil and serve.

62. PIZZA GNOCCHI

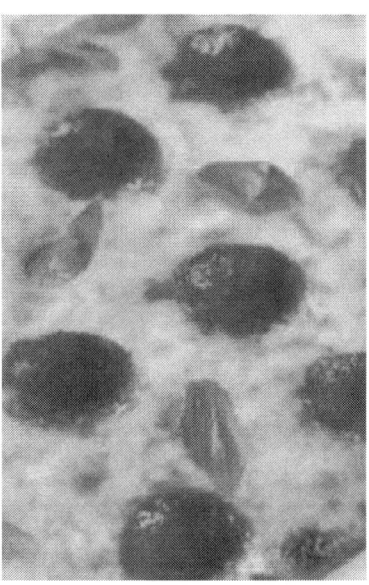

YIELDS: 6 - 8

PREP TIME: 0 HOURS 10 MINS

COOK TIME: 0 HOURS 30 MINS

TOTAL TIME: 0 HOURS 40 MINS

INGREDIENTS

- extra-virgin olive oil
- 32 oz. marinara
- 1 c. ricotta
- 1 tsp. Italian seasoning
- pinch red chili flakes
- Freshly ground black pepper
- kosher salt
- package potato gnocchi

- 2 c. shredded mozzarella (divided)
- 2 tbsp. finely grated Parmesan cheese
- 1/3 c. pepperoni
- 1/4 c. torn basil, for garnish

DIRECTIONS

1. Preheat oven to 350 degrees F. Grease a baking dish with olive oil.
2. In a large bowl, combine marinara, ricotta, red chili flakes and Italian seasoning. Season to taste with salt and pepper. Fold in gnocchi (uncooked) and about 1 cup of mozzarella.
3. Pour sauce and gnocchi mixture into the baking dish. Sprinkle with remaining mozzarella and Parmesan, then place pepperoni on top.
4. Bake for 20-30 minutes until the cheese is melted and the gnocchi is cooked through.
5. Let sit for about 10 minutes. Garnish with basil and serve warm.

63. PIZZA ZUCCHINI BOATS

YIELDS: 8

PREP TIME: 0 HOURS 5 MINS

COOK TIME: 0 HOURS 20 MINS

TOTAL TIME: 0 HOURS 25 MINS

INGREDIENTS

- 4 large zucchini, halved lengthwise
- jar marinara sauce
- 2 c. shredded mozzarella
- 1 c. mini pepperoni
- Chopped fresh basil, for garnish

DIRECTIONS

1. Preheat oven to 350 degrees F. Score zucchini (like you're dicing an avocado) and scoop out insides into a large bowl.
2. In a large skillet over medium heat, heat olive oil. Add zucchini and sauté until tender, 6 to 8 minutes, then pour in marinara.
3. Place hollowed zucchini on a large baking sheet. Spoon on sauce, then top with mozzarella and mini pepperoni. Bake until zucchini is tender and cheese is golden, about 15 minutes.
4. Garnish with basil.

64. GREEK PITA PIZZAS

YIELDS: 4

PREP TIME: 0 HOURS 10 MINS

TOTAL TIME: 0 HOURS 25 MINS

INGREDIENTS

- 2 cloves garlic, minced
- 2 tsp. dried rosemary
- 2 tsp. dried oregano
- 1 tbsp. red wine vinegar
- 3 tbsp. extra-virgin olive oil
- kosher salt
- Freshly ground black pepper
- 1 1/2 c. halved cherry tomatoes
- 1/2 c. chopped cucumber
- 1/3 c. halved kalamata olives
- 2 tbsp. chopped dill
- 1 1/4 c. shredded mozzarella
- 1/2 c. crumbled feta

DIRECTIONS

1. Preheat oven to 350°. In a small bowl, whisk together garlic, dried herbs, vinegar, and oil and season with salt and pepper.
2. In a medium bowl, combine tomatoes, cucumber, olives and dill and pour over most of the vinaigrette. Toss until combined.
3. Brush pitas with remaining vinaigrette and top with mozzarella and feta. Spoon vegetable mixture on top and sprinkle with more mozzarella.
4. Bake until cheese is melty and pita golden, 15 minutes.

65. PIZZAGNA

YIELDS: 8

PREP TIME: 0 HOURS 20 MINS

TOTAL TIME: 1 HOUR 25 MINS

INGREDIENTS

- 1 lb. Lasagna
- 1 tbsp. extra-virgin olive oil
- 1/2 large onion, chopped
- 7 oz. sliced white mushrooms
- 1 lb. ground beef
- 1 tbsp. dried oregano
- 1/4 tsp. crushed red pepper flakes
- 32 oz. marinara
- 3 c. ricotta
- 2 large eggs
- 1 c. freshly grated Parmesan
- kosher salt
- Freshly ground black pepper
- 1 c. pepperoni
- 3 c. shredded mozzarella
- Torn fresh basil, for garnish

DIRECTIONS

1. Preheat oven to 375°. Boil lasagna noodles until al dente.
2. In a saucepan over medium-high heat, heat oil and cook onions and mushrooms until tender. Season with salt. Add ground beef and cook until no longer pink, then stir in oregano and red pepper flakes. Add marinara and stir.
3. Make ricotta mixture: In a medium bowl, stir together ricotta, eggs and Parmesan and season with salt and pepper.
4. Spread a thin layer of sauce in a large baking dish.
5. Top with noodles, ricotta mixture, mozzarella, and a layer of pepperoni. Repeat 2 to 3 times, ending with mozzarella and pepperoni.
6. Cover with foil and bake 35 minutes. Remove foil and bake 10 minutes more.
7. Let sit 20 minutes, then garnish with basil and serve.

66. PIZZA PASTA SALAD

YIELDS: 8

PREP TIME: 0 HOURS 10 MINS

TOTAL TIME: 0 HOURS 20 MINS

INGREDIENTS

- kosher salt
- 1 lb. fusilli

- 1/3 c. extra-virgin olive oil
- 3 tbsp. red wine vinegar
- 1 tbsp. Italian seasoning
- pinch of crushed red pepper flakes
- Freshly ground black pepper
- 1 1/2 c. sliced pepperoni
- 3/4 c. sliced black olives
- 1 large green bell pepper, diced
- 1 1/3 c. freshly grated Parmesan, plus more for garnish

DIRECTIONS

1. In a large pot of salted boiling water, cook fusilli according to package directions until al dente. Drain and transfer to a large bowl.
2. Meanwhile, make dressing: In a small bowl, whisk together olive oil, red wine vinegar, Italian seasoning and crushed red pepper flakes. Season with salt and pepper.
3. Add pepperoni, olives, bell pepper and Parmesan and gently toss. Pour in dressing and toss until combined and well coated.
4. Garnish with additional Parmesan and serve.

67. MARGHERITA PIZZA FRIES

YIELDS: 1

INGREDIENTS

- 16 oz. bag of frozen fries
- 1 pt. cherry tomatoes, halved
- 2 tbsp. olive oil
- kosher salt
- Freshly ground pepper

- 4 oz. fresh marinated mozzarella cut into 1/2-in chunks
- 1/4 oz. Thinly sliced basil

DIRECTIONS

1. Preheat oven to 400 degrees.
2. Add fries to a large ovenproof skillet and cook according to package directions, usually about 25 minutes.
3. Meanwhile toss cherry tomatoes with olive oil and season with salt and pepper to taste. Roast tomatoes for 20 minutes.
4. Top the cooked fries with roasted tomatoes and cheese. Bake for another 10 minutes, until the cheese is melted. Sprinkle with basil.

68. CHEESY BREAKFAST PIZZA

YIELDS: 4

PREP TIME: 0 HOURS 15 MINS

TOTAL TIME: 0 HOURS 50 MINS

INGREDIENTS

- 1 lb. frozen shredded hash browns, defrosted
- 6 large eggs, divided
- 2 c. shredded cheddar, divided
- kosher salt
- Freshly ground black pepper
- Cooking spray, for pan
- 6 strips bacon
- Chopped fresh chives, for garnish

DIRECTIONS

1. Preheat oven to 400°. In a large mixing bowl, combine hash browns, 2 eggs and 1/2 cup cheddar and season with salt and pepper.
2. Spray a baking sheet or pizza pan with cooking spray and add hash brown mixture. Using your hands, pat mixture into a circular crust.
3. Bake until golden, 20 minutes.
4. Meanwhile, in a large skillet over medium heat, cook bacon until crispy, 6 minutes per side. Transfer to a paper towel-lined plate. Drain, then crumble.
5. Top baked crust with remaining 1 1/2 cups cheese and crack remaining 4 eggs on top. Scatter with crumbled bacon and season all over with salt and pepper.
6. Bake until egg whites are set but yolks are runny, 15 minutes. (If you prefer a less runny yolk, bake 18 to 20 minutes.)
7. Garnish with chives, slice, and serve.

69. PRETZEL CRUST PIZZA

PREP TIME: 30 MINS

COOK TIME: 20 MINS

TOTAL TIME: 50 MINS

INGREDIENTS

- 1⅓ cups warm water
- 1 tablespoon active dry yeast
- 2 tablespoons honey

- 3½ cups all purpose flour
- 1 teaspoon salt (regular fine table salt)
- ⅓ cup baking soda
- 1 tablespoon melted butter
- coarse sea salt
- 1 cup pizza sauce
- 1 cup shredded cheese
- pepperoni slices or other desired toppings

DIRECTIONS:

1. Combine warm water, yeast, and honey and stir to mix. Allow to rest for 5 minutes. (If possible, prepare this recipe using a stand mixer)
2. Add flour and 1 teaspoon salt to yeast mixture. Mix until a dough forms. Knead for 5 minutes until dough is smooth and tacky but not too sticky. (If using a stand mixer, use the dough hook to mix and knead dough). Remove dough from bowl and allow to rest on a well-floured surface for 10 minutes.
3. Fill a stock pot (the largest pot you have, at least 10 inches wide) with about 2-3 inches of water. Bring to a boil. Add baking soda - careful, it will bubble and rise. Reduce water to a simmer.
4. Divide dough into three equal portions and roll them out into three 8-inch discs.
5. Gently drop one dough disc into the simmering water. Allow to boil for 30-40 seconds. Use slotted spoons or slotted spatulas to carefully lift dough from the pot and transfer to a paper-towel lined cooling rack (a plate will also work). Repeat with remaining two dough discs.
6. Transfer dough discs to a greased baking sheet (you may need to use more than one baking sheet to fit them all). Brush with melted butter. Sprinkle with coarse sea salt.
7. Bake for 10 minutes at 420. After 10 minutes, top crusts with pizza sauce, cheese, and pepperoni or any other toppings you want. Bake for 10-15 minutes more until cheese is melty and crust is lightly browned. Serve immediately.

70. PEPPERONI PIZZA QUESADILLAS

YIELDS: 4 QUESADILLAS

INGREDIENTS

- 8 flour tortillas (I used Trader Joe's handmade tortillas)
- 8 ounces of shredded mozzarella cheese
- ⅓ lb pepperoni
- 1 16-ounce jar of pizza sauce
- Optional: 1 6-ounce can of sliced black olives, 1 cup of sliced cremini mushrooms

DIRECTIONS:

1. Heat a medium skillet over medium heat and fry the pepperoni until crisp. Transfer on a paper towel to drain.
2. Brush each tortilla with a thin layer of pizza sauce (so thin that if you turned it over, none would drip).
3. Sprinkle cheese on top of the sauce on the bottom tortilla. Top with pepperoni and other toppings, if desired. Sprinkle with another layer of cheese and place the other tortilla on top (sauce side in).
4. Pre-heat a medium cast-iron skilled over medium heat.
5. Lay quesadilla in the pan and cook for 3-5 minutes on each side, until cheese is melted and tortillas are crispy.
6. Slice into quarters and serve with a little bowl of pizza dipping sauce.

71. CLASSIC PEPPERONI PIZZA

PREP TIME: 2 HOURS 20 MINS

COOK TIME: 15 MINS

TOTAL TIME: 2 HOURS 35 MINS

INGREDIENTS

PIZZA CRUST: (FOR THREE 13" PIZZAS)

- ½ c. warm water
- 1¼ c. room temperature water
- 2½ tsp. active yeast
- 1 tsp. sugar
- 1½ tsp. salt
- 2 tbsp. olive oil
- 4 c. all-purpose flour

SAUCE: (FOR THREE 13" PIZZAS)

- 1 (8 oz) can tomato sauce
- 2 tbsp. tomato paste
- 1 tbsp. extra virgin olive oil
- 1 tsp. granulated sugar
- 1 tsp. (1/2 tsp. dried) fresh oregano, chopped
- 1 tsp. (1/2 tsp. dried) fresh basil, chopped

- 1 clove garlic, minced
- Pinch of crushed red pepper flakes
- Salt and freshly ground black pepper

TOPPINGS: (FOR ONE 13" PIZZA)

- 1 tbsp. olive oil
- 2 c. grated mozzarella cheese
- ¼ c. finely grated parmesan cheese
- 30 slices pepperoni
- 2 tbsp fresh basil or oregano leaves
- Pinch of crushed red pepper flakes

DIRECTIONS

1. In a 2-cup liquid measuring cup, add warm water and yeast. Sprinkle sugar over top and allow to sit for 5-7 minutes or until the mixture begins to puff. Add the oil and the room temperature water. Whisk gently to combine.
2. In the bowl of a stand mixer fit with the paddle attachment, combine salt, flour, and water mixture. When dough begins to form a ball, remove paddle attachment and replace with dough hook. With mixing speed on low, knead dough for 2-3 minutes or until a ball begins to form and the dough becomes smooth and elastic.
3. Remove dough from bowl and place in a large well-greased bowl (I prefer using olive oil, but you can also use Pam). Cover bowl tightly with plastic wrap and allow to rise for 2 hours. You can also do a "quick-rise" method and stick the bowl in an oven that has been heated to 200 degrees and then TURNED OFF (that way it's nice and warm in there, but please make sure your oven is actually off before sticking the dough inside). Let it rise for 1 hour.
4. Meanwhile, combine all of the ingredients for the pizza sauce in a small bowl. Refrigerate until needed.
5. To deflate dough, punch with fist. Turn onto a lightly floured surface and divide into two or three balls (depending on how big and how many pizzas you want to make… I make 2). Form into pizza shells to fit the size of your pan (or refrigerate the other dough for up to 48 hours. Place on a lightly greased pan (or one that has been dusted with flour or cornmeal).
6. Preheat oven to 450 degrees. Brush the olive oil over the entire top of the pizza dough. Spread an even layer of pizza sauce over the pizza, leaving about ¾"-1" of dough around edges for the crust. Top with the grated parmesan cheese, then the mozzarella. Place the pepperoni slices on then bake for 12-15 minutes or until the crust is golden brown. Remove from the oven, sprinkle with the red pepper flakes, allow to cool for 10 minutes before topping with basil or oregano (to prevent discoloration and wilting). Slice and serve immediately.

72. PEAR, PROSCIUTTO, AND GORGONZOLA PIZZA

INGREDIENTS

- 1 pound pizza dough
- 1 yellow onion, thinly sliced
- 1/4 t. kosher salt
- 1 t. extra virgin olive oil
- Pinch of salt and pepper
- 1 t. fresh thyme
- 1 pear thinly sliced
- 1/2 cup smoked gouda, shredded
- 1/2 cup part skim mozzarella, shredded
- 1/4 cup gorgonzola, crumbled
- 3 slices of prosciutto, rolled up and sliced thinly

DIRECTIONS:

1. Preheat oven to 450 degrees.
2. Spray a baking sheet or pizza stone with cooking spray.
3. Generously spray a medium sized skillet with cooking spray and heat it over medium high heat.
4. Add the sliced onion and cook the onion until it softens and turns golden brown (about 10 minutes).
5. Roll the pizza dough out onto the sheet or stone.
6. Brush the teaspoon of olive oil all over the top of the dough, then sprinkle on salt, pepper, and the fresh thyme.

7. Sprinkle the shredded cheeses and gorgonzola crumbles all over the pizza.
8. Finish the pizza off by placing the slices of pear, prosciutto, and caramelized onions evenly over the top of the pizza.
9. Bake the pizza for 10-15 minutes or until it is bubbly and golden.
10. Remove from the oven and serve immediately.

NOTES

1. If you don't like smoked gouda, regular gouda or more mozzarella may be used instead.

73. BEST HOMEMADE MARGHERITA PIZZA

YIELD: TWO 10-INCH PIZZAS (2 TO 4 SERVINGS, DEPENDING ON HUNGER LEVEL)

PREP TIME: 20 MINUTES (PLUS 2 HOUR RESTING TIME)

COOK TIME: 15 MINUTES

TOTAL TIME: 45 MINUTES (PLUS 2 HOURS OF RESTING TIME)

INGREDIENTS:

HOMEMADE PIZZA DOUGH:

- 2.5 cups (300 grams) unbleached all-purpose flour
- 1 teaspoon granulated sugar
- 1/2 teaspoon active dry yeast
- 3/4 teaspoon kosher salt
- 7 ounces warm water (105 degrees F – 115 degrees F)
- 1 tablespoon extra virgin olive oil
- 2 tablespoons cornmeal or semolina, for the pizza peel (divided)

PIZZA TOPPINGS:

1. 1 cup pureed or crushed San Marzano (or Italian plum) canned tomatoes
2. 2-3 fresh garlic cloves, minced with a garlic press
3. 1 teaspoon extra virgin olive oil, plus more for drizzling
4. 1/4 teaspoon freshly ground black pepper
5. 2-3 large pinches of kosher salt
6. 2 – 3 tablespoons finely grated parmigiano-reggiano cheese, plus more for serving (I use my microplane)
7. 7 ounces fresh mozzarella cheese, cut into 1/2-inch cubes (*preferably fresh mozzarella not packed in water)
8. 5 – 6 large fresh basil leaves, plus more for garnishing
9. crushed dried red pepper flakes (optional)

DIRECTIONS:

1. Prepare Pizza Dough: In a medium bowl, whisk together the all-purpose flour, sugar, yeast and salt. Add the warm water and olive oil, and stir the mixture with a wooden spoon until the dough just begins to come together. It will seem shaggy and dry, but don't worry.
2. Scrape the dough onto a well-floured counter top and knead the dough for three minutes. It should quickly come together and begin to get sticky. Dust the dough with flour as needed (sometimes I will have to do this 2 to 3 times, depending on humidity levels) – it should be slightly tacky, but should not be sticking to your counter top. After three minutes, the dough should be smooth, slightly elastic, and tacky. Lightly grease a large mixing bowl with olive oil, and place the dough into the bowl.
3. Cover the bowl with a kitchen towel (or plastic wrap) and allow the dough to rise in a warm, dry area of your kitchen for 2 hours or until the dough has doubled in size. If your kitchen is very cold, one great tip that I do all the time is to heat a large heatproof measuring cup of water in the microwave for 2-3 minutes. This creates a nice warm environment and I'll immediately

remove the cup and place the bowl with the dough in the microwave until it has risen. [If you are preparing in advance, see the note section for freezing instructions.]

4. Preheat Oven and Pizza Stone: Place the pizza stone on the center (or top third) rack of your oven, and preheat the oven and pizza stone to 550 degrees Fahrenheit (for at least 30-45 minutes). If your oven does not go up to 550 degrees, heat it to the absolute maximum temperature that it can go. If it can heat to higher than 550 degrees Fahrenheit, even better!
5. As the oven is preheating, assemble the ingredients. In a small bowl, stir together the pureed tomatoes, minced garlic, extra virgin olive oil, pepper, and salt. Set aside another small bowl with the cubed mozzarella cheese (pat the cheese with a paper towel to remove any excess moisture). Set aside the basil leaves and grated parmigiano-reggiano cheese for easy grabbing.
6. Separate the dough into two equal-sized portions. It will deflate slightly, but that is OK. Place the dough on a large plate or floured counter top, cover gently with plastic wrap, and allow the dough to rest for 5 to 10 minutes.
7. Assemble the Pizza: Sprinkle the pizza peel (alternatively, you can use the back of a baking sheet – but it will be harder!) with a tablespoon of the cornmeal. Gently stretch one ball of pizza dough into roughly a 10-inch circle (don't worry if its not perfectly uniform). If the dough springs back or is too elastic, allow it to rest for an additional five minutes. The edges of the dough can be slightly thicker, but make sure the center of the dough is thin (you should be able to see some light through it if you held it up). Gently transfer the dough onto the cornmeal-dusted pizza peel or baking sheet.
8. Drizzle or brush the dough lightly with olive oil (teaspoon or so). Using a large spoon, add roughly 1/2 cup of the tomato sauce onto the pizza dough, leaving a 1/2-inch or 3/4-inch border on all sides. Use the back of the spoon to spread it evenly and thinly. Sprinkle a tablespoon of parmigiano-reggiano cheese onto the pizza sauce. Add half of the cubed mozzarella, distributing it evenly over the entire pizza. Using your hands, tear a few large basil leaves, and sprinkle the basil over the pizza. At this point, I'll occasionally stretch the sides of the dough out a bit to make it even thinner. Gently slide the pizza from the peel onto the heated baking stone. Bake for 7 to 8 minutes, or until the crust is golden and the cheese is bubbling and caramelized and the edges of the pizza are golden brown. Remove the pizza carefully from the oven with the pizza peel, transfer to a wooden cutting board or foil, drizzle the top with olive oil, some grated parmigiano-reggiano cheese, and chiffonade of fresh basil. Slice and serve immediately and/or prepare the second pizza.
9. If you're serving two pizzas at once, I recommend placing the cooked pizza on a separate baking sheet while you prepare the other pizza. In the last few minutes of cooking, place the prepared pizza into the oven (on a rack below the pizza stone) so that it is extra hot for serving. Otherwise, I recommend serving one pizza fresh out of the oven, keeping the oven hot, and preparing the second pizza after people have gone through the first one! The pizza will taste great either way, but it is at its prime within minutes out of the oven!

74. BUFFALO CHICKEN PIZZA

PREP TIME: 10 MINS

COOK TIME: 7 MINS

YIELD: 1 LARGE PIZZA

INGREDIENTS

- 1 10-ounce ball pizza dough
- ¼ cup pizza sauce (See our recipe here or your favorite jarred sauce)
- 2 tablespoons Frank's RedHot Sauce
- 2 tablespoons blue cheese dressing
- ½ cup Monterey Jack cheese
- ¼ cup Fontina cheese
- ¼ blue cheese
- ¾ Pulled Buffalo Chicken
- Additional drizzle of Frank's RedHot Sauce
- Flour for dusting
- Corn meal to coat pizza peel
- Pizza stone

DIRECTIONS:

1. Bring dough ball to room temperature on a floured pan. Cover dough ball with plastic and a dish towel and let sit in a warm place for 30 minutes. The link to our perfect pizza dough makes six 7-ounce pizza balls and this recipe is for a 10 ounce ball so you will need to make adjustments.
2. On a floured surface, flatten dough to a 12-14 inch round. Cover with plastic and dish towel again and let sit for another 30 minutes.
3. While dough is sitting, mix pizza sauce with the two tablespoons of hot sauce.
4. Preheat oven to 500 degrees with pizza stone.
5. On a pizza peel, sprinkle corn meal and place prepared dough circle on corn meal.
6. Spoon prepared pizza sauce onto dough coming about a half inch from edge.
7. Drizzle blue cheese dressing over sauce.
8. In a small bowl, mix three cheeses and sprinkle over sauce.
9. Spread Pulled Buffalo Chicken over cheese.
10. Slide onto the hot pizza stone and cook seven minutes. Check bottom of pizza and cook for one more minute if needed. Slide out onto a cutting board and drizzle some additional hot sauce over top.
11. Cut and serve.

75. HAWAIIAN BBQ CHICKEN PIZZA

YIELD: 1 12-INCH PIZZA

INGREDIENTS

- 1 lb pizza dough , homemade or store bought
- 12 oz boneless skinless chicken breasts
- 2 Tbsp olive oil , divided
- 3/4 cup barbecue sauce , divided
- 4 slices bacon , cooked and chopped
- 2 cups (8 oz) low-moisture mozzarella, shredded
- 1 cup chopped fresh pineapple (chop into small pieces)
- 1/3 of a medium red onion , sliced thin and run under cool water to remove harsh bite
- 1/4 cup cilantro , chopped or torn
- 1 cloves garlic , minced
- Freshly ground black pepper

DIRECTIONS:

1. Preheat oven to 475 degrees.
2. Preheat a grill to medium-high heat. Brush both sides of chicken lightly with 1 Tbsp of the olive oil and season both sides with salt and pepper. Grill until cooked through, rotating once halfway through cooking, and brushing with 3 Tbsp of the barbecue sauce during last 1 - 2 minutes of grilling. Remove from grill and set aside to cool 5 minutes.
3. Spread pizza dough out on a floured sheet of parchment paper over a pizza tray to a 12-inch round (if you prefer a crisp crust, preheat a pizza stone in oven and transfer pizza on parchment using a pizza peel to preheated stone). In a mixing bowl whisk together remaining olive oil and garlic. Brush entire surface of dough with olive oil mixture and let rest 10 minutes.
4. Cut chicken into cubes. Brush dough with remaining barbecue sauce (1/2 cup + 1 Tbsp). Top with 1/3 of the mozzarella then top with chicken, pineapple, bacon and red onion. Sprinkle with remaining mozzarella and season with freshly ground black pepper. Bake in preheated oven until crust is golden, about 11 - 13 minutes. Slice and serve warm topped with cilantro.

76. WISCONSIN BEER CHEESE SAUCE BACON PIZZA

INGREDIENTS

- 1 roll of Traditional White Bread Rhodes Dough
- 3 TBSPs unsalted butter divided
- 1 large yellow onion
- 1 tsp apple cider vinegar
- 1/2 lb spicy Italian sausage (I used "Jennie-O turkey sausage")
- 1/2 lb bacon diced
- 2 cloves garlic minced
- 1/2 tsp salt
- 1/2 tsp paprika
- 1/2 tsp ground mustard
- 2 TBSP flour
- 1/2 cup beer
- 1/2 cup heavy cream
- 1 1/2 cups finely shredded cheddar jack cheese

DIRECTIONS:

1. The night before, set out your Rhodes dough in a large bowl and cover with plastic wrap to defrost.
2. The day of, preheat your oven to 375 degrees.
3. Melt 1 tablespoon of butter in a heavy bottomed pan or cast iron skillet, over medium heat.
4. While it's melting, slice up the onion. Toss it in the pan over the melted butter and let stand about five minutes. Scrape up the onions and the bottom of the pan each five minutes until the

onions are completely caramelized, about a half hour. Then add the apple cider vinegar to the bottom of the pan for the deglazing. Remove the onions from the pan.
5. Add the Italian sausage to the pan (no need to clean in between) and cook until completely done, breaking it up as you go. Remove from the pan and set aside.
6. Add the bacon to the pan (no need to clean in between) and cook until crisp. Remove from the pan and set aside.
7. Spread the thawed dough onto a large pizza stone or baking pan. Poke it a few times with a fork and put it into the oven for 22 minutes.
8. While the dough is baking, melt the remaining 2 tablespoons of butter in a small saucepan over medium low heat. Add some minced garlic to the pan, stirring. Add the paprika, salt, and ground mustard.
9. Then add 2 tablespoons of all purpose flour, whisking it into the butter until fully combined. Let the mixture cook about a minute, until it begins to smell nutty and deepens in color. Then slowly whisk in the 1/2 cup of beer, adding just a little at a time to fully combine it to the flour/butter mixture.
10. Once the beer is completely added, slowly mix in the heavy cream. Raise the temperature on the pan and bring to a boil. Once at a boil, bring the temperature back down and simmer, while stirring for five minutes.
11. Remove the sauce from the heat and stir in the cup and a half of cheese just a little at a time.
12. Take the dough out of the oven and allow it to sit for a few minutes so it isn't pipping hot.
13. Spread the cheese sauce over the cooked dough (you may not use all of it), then add the bacon, sausage, and finally the caramelized onions. Slice and serve!

77. CHEESEBURGER PIZZA

PREP TIME: 20 MINS

COOK TIME: 12 MINS

TOTAL TIME: 32 MINS

INGREDIENTS

- 1/2 cup ketchup
- 2 tablespoons yellow mustard
- 3/4 pound lean ground beef
- 1/3 cup diced onion
- 1/3 cup diced green pepper
- 1/2 teaspoon kosher salt
- 1/4 teaspoon steak seasoning
- 1 prebaked thin pizza crust, such as Boboli
- 6 slices bacon, cooked and crumbled
- 1/4 cup diced dill pickle
- 1 cup shredded cheddar
- 1 cup shredded mozzarella
- 2 roma tomatoes, thinly sliced

DIRECTIONS:

1. Preheat oven to 425 degrees. Place a pizza stone in the oven if you have one.
2. In a small bowl mix together ketchup and mustard to make sauce.
3. In a large skillet, sauté ground beef for 3 to 4 minutes, breaking the meat up with a wooden spoon. Add onion and green pepper and continue to cook until meat is no longer pink. Spoon off any excess grease.
4. Add salt and steak seasoning to ground beef mixture. Mix 1 tablespoon of sauce into ground beef mixture.
5. Spread some sauce on the pizza crust. I just add a thin layer of sauce. You can always drizzle additional sauce on top of the pizza.
6. Sprinkle half of the cheddar cheese and half of the mozzarella cheese on top of the sauce.
7. Spoon the ground beef mixture onto the pizza crust and sprinkle with bacon and pickles.
8. Top with remaining cheese and roma tomato slices.
9. Place on baking stone, directly on oven rack, or on a baking sheet and bake for 10-12 minutes, or until cheese is melted.

78. PEPPERONI PIZZA POT PIE

PREP TIME: 20 MINS

COOK TIME: 35 MINS

TOTAL TIME: 55 MINS

INGREDIENTS

- butter to grease the cast iron skillet
- 2 packages store bought fresh or frozen pizza dough, rolled out flat
- ½ to 1 cup tomato sauce
- ½ small onion, sliced
- ½ cup cremini mushrooms, sliced
- ¼ cup green olives, sliced
- 1 teaspoon crushed red chili pepper flakes; optional for some heat
- 1- 2 cups pepperoni
- 2 - 2½ cups shredded mozzarella cheese
- 1 egg + ½ teaspoon water, slightly beaten for egg wash
- Special equipment suggested:
- cast iron skillet

DIRECTIONS:

1. Preheat your oven to 400 degrees F. Grease the inside of a 12-inch cast-iron skillet with the butter. Using your rolling pin, transfer the first rolled out pizza dough to the center of the cast iron skillet and spread evenly on the bottom and up the sides; only as high or thick as you want your pizza pie to be.
2. Spread on the tomato sauce, top with your sliced vegetables, and sprinkle on the crushed red chili pepper flakes if using.
3. Cover the entire top of the pizza with the pepperoni. Top with the shredded mozzarella cheese and transfer the second rolled out pizza dough to the top of the pizza pie, connecting the dough to the edges all around the skillet (you can cut off any excess dough if necessary). Using your fingers or a fork, make indentations around the edge of the pizza dough. Make four slits (openings) into the center of the pizza pie to allow steam to escape and lightly brush on the egg wash over the entire top of the pizza pot pie.
4. Bake for 30-35 minutes or until the crust is golden brown and cooked through and you can see the cheese bubbling through the cuts. Remove from the oven and allow to cool for at least 5-10 minutes. Slice, serve and enjoy!

79. PIZZA CAKE

PREP TIME: 20 MIN

COOK TIME: 40 MIN

TOTAL TIME: 1 HOUR

INGREDIENTS

- 2 cans Pillsbury™ refrigerated classic pizza crust
- 1 1/2 cups Muir Glen™ organic pizza sauce (from 15-oz can)
- 3 cups shredded mozzarella cheese (12 oz)
- 1 cup sliced pepperoni
- 1 tablespoon butter, if desired

DIRECTIONS:

1. Preheat oven to 400 degrees F.
2. Measure diameter of tall-sided ovenproof pan. (Pan used was 6-inch in diameter with 4-inch high side.) Unroll 1 can of dough onto work surface; press out into thin layer. Cut out 3 (6-inch) rounds; place on cookie sheet. Bake 8 minutes. Remove from cookie sheet to cooling rack; cool.
3. Unroll remaining can of dough; cut 2 additional (6-inch) rounds from long edge of dough, leaving opposite side untouched. Place rounds on cooled cookie sheet. Bake 8 minutes. Remove from cookie sheet; cool.
4. Meanwhile, line pan with cooking parchment paper so that ends of paper stick up and out of pan. Cut long strip of dough at least 1/2 inch wider than height of pan. Carefully drape long strip of dough around inside edge of pan to line, leaving 1/2 inch hanging over outside edge of pan and bottom of pan open. Pinch seam to seal.
5. Carefully place 1 partially baked crust round in bottom of pan. Spread pizza sauce over crust; top with pepperoni slices and sprinkle with mozzarella cheese (when cheese melts, crust above will stick to it). Repeat to make 3 more layers. For top layer, place last crust over cheese; sprinkle with remaining cheese and arrange remaining pepperoni on top.
6. Fold overhanging dough over top layer of pizza cake to make a raised crust edge.
7. Bake 20 to 25 minutes or until dough around pizza cake is fully cooked. (To test, carefully pull up parchment paper to raise pizza cake out of pan.) Once completely baked, cool in pan 5 minutes. Remove pizza cake from pan; brush crust with butter. Use sharp knife to cut slices like you would a cake.

80. APPLE CHEDDAR PIZZA WITH CARAMELIZED ONIONS & WALNUTS

PREP TIME: 10 MINUTES

COOK TIME: 1 HOUR 30 MINUTES

TOTAL TIME: 1 HOUR 40 MINUTES

YIELD: 4-6 SERVINGS

INGREDIENTS

- 1 tbsp. olive oil
- 1 large yellow onion, thinly sliced
- salt + pepper to taste
- 1 tbsp. butter
- 1 apple, cored and thinly sliced (Braeburn, Fuji, or Honeycrisp work well)
- 1 tbsp. maple syrup
- 1 large prepared pizza crust
- 1 c. shredded aged cheddar cheese
- 2 tbsp chopped walnuts

DIRECTIONS:

1. Heat oil in a large skillet over low heat. Add onion and cook until caramelized, stirring every 5 minutes or so at first and then, as the onions begin to brown, more frequently. This could take from 30 minutes to over an hour, depending on your stove. Season with salt and pepper and remove from heat.
2. Preheat oven to temperature indicated on pizza crust package.
3. Wipe skillet clean; add butter and melt over medium heat. Once butter has melted, add apple slices and saute for about 10 minutes, or until softened, stirring frequently. Stir in maple syrup and continue cooking until liquid has evaporated. Remove from heat.
4. Top pizza crust with caramelized onions, shredded cheese, apples, and walnuts. Bake for time indicated on package or until cheese has melted.

NOTES

1. Make the caramelized onions in advance to shorten the cook time. If the instructions on your pizza crust indicate that it should be baked at a higher temperature than 375 degrees or for longer than 10 minutes, toast walnuts separately and add them to pizza after it's finished baking.

81. GARLIC-RANCH CHICKEN PIZZA

PREP TIME: 5 MINS

COOK TIME: 12 MINS

TOTAL TIME: 17 MINS

INGREDIENTS

FOR THE PIZZA:

- Dough for one large pizza
- 2 cups shredded mozzarella cheese
- 1/2 cup bacon, cooked and crumbled
- 1 cup cooked chicken, shredded
- 2 tomatoes thinly sliced

FOR THE GARLIC-RANCH SAUCE:

- 2 Tablespoons sour cream
- 3 Tablespoons mayonnaise
- 2 1/2 Tablespoons milk
- 1/2 teaspoon garlic salt
- 1/8 teaspoon dill weed
- 1/8 teaspoon dried parsley flakes
- dash of onion powder
- salt and freshly ground black pepper to taste

DIRECTIONS:

1. Mix all ingredients together for the garlic-ranch sauce. Spread mixture over the top of the pizza dough.
2. Sprinkle 1 cup of the mozzarella cheese over top, followed by the chicken, bacon, and tomatoes. Sprinkle remaining cheese on top.
3. Bake at 450 degrees F for 9-12 minutes, or until crust is golden brown and cheese is bubbly.

FOR GRILLED PIZZAS:

1. Oil your grill and turn heat to medium-low. Shape dough into long, slipper-shaped pieces.
2. Brush dough with olive oil and grill for 2 minutes on one side, with the grill cover on.
3. Flip to the other side and brush again with olive oil. Cook for 2 minutes, with the grill lid on.
4. Remove crust to a plate and add toppings.
5. Return to grill and cook just until cheese is melted, 1-2 more minutes.

82. CHICKEN ALFREDO PIZZA

INGREDIENTS

- 1 pound pizza dough
- 2 t. extra virgin olive oil
- 2 T. shallots, minced
- 1 clove of garlic, minced
- 1/2 t. kosher salt
- 1/4 t. black pepper
- 2 1/2 t. flour
- 3/4 cup skim milk, room temperature
- 1 cup part skim mozzarella cheese, shredded
- 3/4 cup fontina cheese, shredded
- 1 cup cooked chicken breast, sliced
- 1 T. flat leaf parsley, chopped

DIRECTIONS:

1. Preheat oven to 450 degrees and spray a baking sheet or pizza stone with cooking spray.
2. In a small saucepan over medium high heat, heat the oil.
3. When the oil is hot add in the shallot and cook for 1 minute.
4. Add in the garlic, salt, and pepper and cook for another 30 seconds.
5. Add in the flour and whisk everything together cooking for another 30 seconds.
6. Slowly pour in the milk whisking the sauce as you pour.

7. Continue to whisk the sauce for another 2-3 minutes until the sauce has thickened.
8. Pour the sauce over the top of the pizza dough.
9. Top the pizza with the mozzarella and fontina cheese and the sliced chicken.
10. Bake for 10-15 minutes until the crust is golden and the cheese is bubbly.
11. Remove from the oven and top with the chopped parsley, serve immediately.

83. PIZZA HOMEMADE "HOT POCKETS"

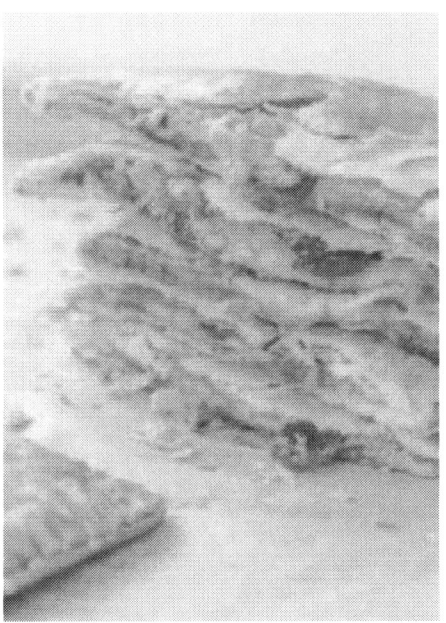

YIELDS: 4

PREP TIME: 0 HOURS 30 MINS

TOTAL TIME: 0 HOURS 30 MINS

INGREDIENTS

- 1 lb. store-bought or homemade pie crust
- 1/2 c. marinara
- 1 1/2 c. shredded mozzarella
- 1/2 c. mini pepperoni
- 1 large egg, beaten with 1 tbsp. water

DIRECTIONS

1. Preheat oven to 350 degrees F and line a baking sheet with parchment paper. On a floured work surface, roll out pie crust into a large rectangle and slice off rounded edges (if using store-bought). Slice into four strips.
2. Spoon marinara over bottom half of strips and top with mozzarella and pepperoni. Fold over tops.
3. Use your fingers to pinch to seal and press the twines of a fork to crimp. Brush with egg wash and transfer to prepared baking sheet.
4. Bake until golden and puffy, 18 to 20 minutes.

84. CHICKEN FAJITA PIZZA

PREP TIME: 15 MINS

COOK TIME: 15 MINS

TOTAL TIME: 30 MINS

INGREDIENTS

- 1/2 pizza dough
- 2 cups shredded chicken I used one breast from a rotisserie chicken
- 1 large onion sliced
- 1 green bell pepper julienned
- 2 tbsp olive oil

- 1/4 tsp salt
- 1/4 tsp pepper
- 1 tsp chili powder
- 1 cup salsa
- 1 1/2 cups shredded Mexican cheese blend
- 1 cup shredded Mozzarella cheese

DIRECTIONS:

1. Preheat oven to 500 F degrees.
2. Roll out the pizza dough and place on a pizza baking pan, or a pizza stone.
3. In a large skillet, saute the onion and pepper in the olive oil until onion is slightly caramelized. Season with salt, pepper and chili powder. Add shredded chicken and toss everything together.
4. Spread salsa over the crust. Top with mozzarella cheese. Top with the chicken mixture evenly over the entire pizza. Top with the Mexican cheese blend.
5. Bake for 10 to 15 minutes or until cheese is bubbly and crust is golden brown.

85. EASY PIZZA CASSEROLE

INGREDIENTS

- 3 3/4 cup Bisquick
- 1 cup water
- 1 tsp garlic powder
- 1 1/2 teaspoon Italian Seasoning

- 1 (14-15 oz) jar pizza sauce
- 6 oz sliced pepperoni
- 2 cups shredded mozzarella cheese

DIRECTIONS:

1. Preheat oven to 375°
2. Spray a 9×13 baking dish lightly with cooking spray, set aside.
3. In a medium bowl combine Bisquick, garlic powder and Italian seasonings. Add water and stir until a soft dough forms. (If dough is too sticky, sprinkle a few tablespoons more Bisquick, if it feels dry add a tablespoon of water). Divide dough in half and drop dough by tablespoon sized portions all over the bottom of the prepared pan. Pan will not be covered by the dough. Next drizzle 1 cup of the pizza sauce on top of the dough. Then layer half of the pepperoni on top of sauce. Finally sprinkle half of the mozzarella cheese all over the pepperoni. Repeat this entire process again with remaining ingredients.
4. Bake 20-25 minutes. Cut into squares and serve warm.

86. SPINACH ARTICHOKE PIZZA

INGREDIENTS

- 1 (16 oz) homemade or store bought pizza dough
- 8 oz fresh spinach , divided
- 2 Tbsp butter
- 2 Tbsp all-purpose flour
- 3/4 cup milk

- 1/4 tsp onion powder
- Salt and freshly ground black pepper
- 1 clove garlic , minced
- 2 Tbsp extra virgin olive oil , divided
- 4 oz provolone cheese (1 cup. I used deli slices and chopped)
- 2 oz shredded low-moisture mozzarella cheese (1/2 cup)
- 2 oz finely shredded parmesan cheese (slightly packed 1/2 cup)
- 6 - 8 canned artichoke hearts , drained well and quartered (don't use marinated)
- Red pepper flakes , for serving (optional)

DIRECTIONS:

1. Preheat oven to 450 degrees. Place pizza stone in preheated oven and allow to rest in oven 20 minutes. Meanwhile, stretch and shape pizza dough over a sheet of parchment paper to a 13-inch round, while creating a taller rim along outer edge. Brush with 1 Tbsp olive oil and season crust lightly with salt and freshly ground black pepper, then allow to rest while pizza stone preheats (note that if your pizza crust has been refrigerated, be sure to bring it to room temperature first, then shape and let it rest the 20 minutes).
2. In a large saucepan, heat remaining 1 Tbsp olive oil over medium-high heat. Once oil is hot, add 3/4 of the spinach and saute just until wilted. Transfer to a layer of paper towels and gently press some of the excess liquid out. Finely chop spinach and set aside.
3. In a small saucepan, melt butter over medium heat, then while whisking add in flour and onion powder and cook 2 minutes, stirring constantly. Then while whisking slowly stir in milk and increase temperature to medium-high heat and cook, stirring constantly until mixture has thickened well. Season with salt and pepper to taste. Remove from heat and stir in minced garlic and sautéed, chopped spinach. Chop remaining fresh spinach (you should have about 1 1/2 cups chopped), set aside.
4. To assemble pizza, spread the spinach béchamel sauce (the white sauce) evenly over pizza crust, leaving the rim uncoated. Sprinkle chopped, fresh spinach over sauce followed by provolone, mozzarella and parmesan cheeses and chopped artichokes. Slide a pizza peel under parchment paper and carefully transfer pizza to hot pizza stone in oven. Bake 10 - 13 minutes until crust is golden brown. Cut into slices and serve warm sprinkled with red pepper flakes to taste if desired.

87. RANCH PIZZA WITH WHITE CHEDDAR AND PROSCIUTTO

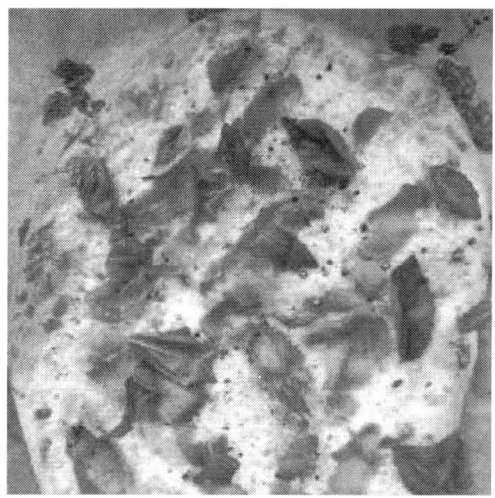

YIELDS: 4

PREP TIME: 0 HOURS 20 MINS

TOTAL TIME: 0 HOURS 30 MINS

INGREDIENTS

- 1 tbsp. unsalted butter
- 1 tbsp. all-purpose flour
- 1 c. whole milk
- 2 tbsp. "Hidden Valley® Original Ranch® Dips Mix"
- kosher salt
- Freshly ground black pepper
- 5 tbsp. extra-virgin olive oil, plus more for baking sheet
- 8 oz. pizza dough, at room temperature
- 4 oz. sharp white cheddar, grated
- 4 oz. thinly sliced prosciutto
- Fresh basil, for serving

DIRECTIONS

1. Melt butter in small saucepan over medium heat until foamy. Whisk in flour and cook, whisking, 1 minute. Whisk in milk and bring to boil. Reduce heat to simmer and continue to cook, whisking occasionally, until thick like heavy cream, about 5 minutes. Whisk in "Hidden Valley®Original Ranch® Dips Mix" and season with salt and pepper. Set aside to cool.

2. Preheat oven to 450 degrees F with bottom rack set in lowest position. Line rimmed baking sheet with parchment paper and lightly brush paper with oil. Stretch dough into large oval shape and place on baking sheet; set aside.
3. Spread ranch sauce over pizza dough and top with cheese and prosciutto. Bake until cheese is melted and crust is golden brown, 12 to 15 minutes. Season with black pepper and basil.

88. PIZZA PULL-APART BREAD

YIELDS: 10

PREP TIME: 0 HOURS 10 MINS

COOK TIME: 0 HOURS 20 MINS

TOTAL TIME: 0 HOURS 30 MINS

INGREDIENTS

- 1 stick butter, melted
- 1 tbsp. Italian seasoning (in the spice aisle)
- 1 loaf crusty bread, like Italian or sourdough
- 2 c. shredded mozzarella
- 2 c. pepperoni slices
- Marinara or pizza sauce, for dipping

DIRECTIONS

1. Preheat oven to 350 degrees F. In small bowl, mix together butter and Italian seasoning. Set aside.
2. Slice top of bread long-ways and then cross-ways, being careful not to cut loaf all the way through. Gently open cuts of loaf.
3. Pour butter mixture all over bread, making sure mixture makes it into crevices. Then cover bread with cheese and pepperoni, pushing both deep into cuts, as well.
4. Move loaf to sheet pan, and bake for 20 minutes, until cheese is melted. Serve immediately with warm marinara sauce for dipping.

89. MEXICAN PIZZA FOR JUNE DAIRY MONTH

PREP TIME: 15 MINUTES

COOK TIME: 10 MINUTES

YIELD: 6 SERVINGS

INGREDIENTS

- 1 lb. lean ground beef
- 1 envelope (1.25 oz.) taco seasoning (or use homemade)
- 12 taco-size flour tortillas
- 1 can (16 oz.) refried beans (or use homemade)
- 1 can (10 oz.) enchilada sauce (or use homemade)

- 2 cups (8 oz.) Cheddar cheese, shredded
- 1 medium tomato, chopped
- 3 green onions, chopped
- 1 can (2.25 oz.) sliced black olives
- Sour cream, for serving (optional)

DIRECTIONS:

1. Brown and crumble ground beef in a large skillet over medium-high heat. Drain if necessary. Add the packet of taco seasoning and ¾ cup water. Bring to boil. Reduce heat and simmer 5 minutes, stirring occasionally until most of the water has evaporated. Set beef mixture aside.
2. Spread about ⅓-cup of the beans onto 6 tortillas. Top each bean tortilla with some of the beef mixture, dividing the beef evenly between the tortillas. Spread the beef evenly over the beans. Top each bean and meat tortilla with a plain tortilla.
3. Preheat oven to 500°F.
4. Heat a skillet or griddle over medium-high heat. Place pizzas in skillet and cook for 3-5 minutes or until golden brown. Carefully flip the pizzas over and cook an additional 3-5 minutes or until golden brown. Remove the pizzas to a large baking sheet. Repeat with remaining pizzas.
5. Top each pizza with enchilada sauce. Sprinkle with ⅓ cup cheese. Top with tomatoes, green onions and black olives. Bake pizzas for 3-5 minutes or until the cheese is melted and the pizza is heated through.
6. To serve, slice pizza into fourths with a pizza cutter. Serve with sour cream, if desired.

90. BEET PESTO PIZZA WITH KALE AND GOAT CHEESE

PREP TIME: 1 HOUR

COOK TIME: 30 MINUTES

TOTAL TIME: 1 HOUR 30 MINUTES

INGREDIENTS

- 1 lb gluten-free pizza dough
- 1 cup beet pesto
- 2 cups kale leaves thinly sliced*
- 1.5 cups mozzarella cheesegrated
- 2 ounces goat cheese

DIRECTIONS:

1. Prepare the beet pesto and the pizza dough.
2. Preheat the oven to 415 degrees F.
3. Dust gluten-free flour (or cornmeal) on a baking sheet and press or roll the dough to desired thickness.
4. Bake the dough for 5 to 7 minutes with no toppings.
5. Remove the crust from the oven and spread the beet pesto over it. Add the kale leaves, followed by the goat cheese and mozarella. Note: the kale will cook down in the oven.
6. Bake pizza for 20 to 25 minutes or to desired crisp.
7. Allow pizza to cool 5 minutes before serving.

91. COBB SALAD PIZZA

6 SERVINGS

PREP TIME: 0 HOURS 20 MINS

COOK TIME: 0 HOURS 15 MINS

TOTAL TIME: 0 HOURS 35 MINS

INGREDIENTS

- pizza dough (about 1/2 lb)
- 1/2 c. mozzarella, sliced
- 1/4 c. extra-virgin olive oil
- 1/2 tsp. Flaky sea salt (such as Maldon)
- 1 tsp. Dijon mustard
- 1 tsp. oney
- 2 tbsp. balsamic vinegar
- 1 c. chopped romaine lettuce
- 2 hard-boiled eggs, halved
- 1 avocado, sliced
- 1 c. grilled chicken, chopped
- 2 slices cooked bacon, chopped
- 1/2 c. crumbed goat cheese
- ground pepper

DIRECTIONS

1. Preheat oven to 500 degrees F.
2. Stretch pizza dough to form a large circle. Scatter mozzarella on top and drizzle with olive oil. Sprinkle with flaky sea salt, if desired.
3. Bake for 15 minutes or until the crust is golden brown and the cheese is bubbly.
4. Meanwhile, make vinaigrette. Mix together the mustard, honey and balsamic vinegar. Slowly drizzle in the olive oil and whisk until the dressing emulsifies. Adjust seasoning according to taste.
5. Top the pizza dough, starting with the lettuce. Drizzle the lettuce with some of the vinaigrette.
6. Form spirals, starting from the center of the pizza, with the tomatoes, eggs and avocado slices. Scatter the chicken, bacon and goat cheese evenly on top. Drizzle more vinaigrette on top. Add freshly ground pepper.

92. PIZZA WITH SWISS CHARD, SAUSAGE, AND MOZZARELLA

YIELDS: 4

PREP TIME: 0 HOURS 20 MINS

TOTAL TIME: 0 HOURS 35 MINS

INGREDIENTS

- 2 tbsp. extra-virgin olive oil
- 2 Italian sausages, casings removed
- 2 garlic cloves, minced
- 2 bunches Swiss chard, chopped
- kosher salt
- Freshly ground black pepper
- 1/4 c. cornmeal
- 1 ball fresh pizza dough (if frozen, make sure it's thawed)
- 4 oz. fresh mozzarella, thinly sliced
- 1/2 c. freshly grated Parmesan
- 1 tsp. Crushed red pepper flakes, for garnish

DIRECTIONS

1. Preheat oven to 450° and lightly grease a baking sheet with 1 tablespoon olive oil, then set aside.

2. In a large skillet over medium-high heat, heat remaining 1 tablespoon olive oil. Cook sausage, breaking up with a spoon, until crumbly and lightly browned, 7 to 8 minutes, then transfer to a paper towel-lined plate.
3. Pour all but 1 tablespoon oil from pan, then add garlic and cook over medium-high heat until fragrant, 1 minute. Add chard in two batches, stirring until wilted, 4 minutes. Season with salt and pepper, then transfer to a colander to drain.
4. Spread cornmeal onto a clean work surface, roll out dough into a large oval or rectangle, and transfer to a greased baking sheet. Add half the mozzarella, sausage, and Swiss chard, then top with remaining mozzarella and Parmesan.
5. Bake pizza until crust is golden brown and cheese is bubbly, about 15 minutes. Sprinkle with red pepper flakes, season with salt and pepper, and cut into pieces.

93. EASY DINNER IDEA: 10 MINUTE MAC AND CHEESE PIZZA

INGREDIENTS:

- 1 8 inch pre-baked (mini) pizza crust
- 1 Horizon Macaroni and Mild Cheddar cup
- 1/4 cup shredded cheese (I used a white cheddar mozzarella blend)
- 1 tsp bacon crumbles (optional)
- pinch of parmesan and Italian spice blend for garnish

DIRECTIONS:

1. Preheat oven to 450 degrees.
2. Prepare the macaroni and cheese according to package directions.
3. Spread mac and cheese over the crust.
4. Top with extra cheese, parmesan, Italian Spice blend and optional bacon crumbles.
5. Bake for 8 to 12 minutes or until everything is hot and bubbly.
6. Serve and Enjoy!

94. PHILLY CHEESESTEAK PIZZA

INGREDIENTS

- 1 recipe of your favorite pizza crust
- ¼ cup mayonnaise
- ½ pound cooked and chopped steak
- ¼ cup chopped sweet onion
- A handful of green and red pepper strips
- 1 and ½ cups shredded provolone cheese
- 1 and ½ cups mozzarella cheese

DIRECTIONS:

1. Preheat oven to 400 F. Shape crust into a 12 inch circle. Spread the mayonnaise on the base of the crust. Top with steak, onion, peppers, and cheeses. Bake for 15-20 minutes or until lightly browned.

95. SUN-DRIED TOMATO AND ARUGULA PIZZA

YIELDS: 8

COOK TIME: 1 HOUR 0 MINS

TOTAL TIME: 2 HOURS 30 MINS

INGREDIENTS

DOUGH

- 4 c. all-purpose flour
- 1 tbsp. sugar
- 1 tsp. active dry yeast
- 1 1/4 c. warm water
- 3 tbsp. extra-virgin olive oil
- 1 tsp. salt

TOPPINGS

- 32 sun-dried tomato halves
- 4 clove garlic
- c. extra-virgin olive oil
- 1 lb. fresh mozzarella
- salt
- Freshly ground pepper
- 2 c. packed baby arugula

DIRECTIONS

1. In the bowl of a standing mixer fitted with the dough hook, mix the flour, sugar, and yeast at medium speed. At low speed, stir in half of the warm water, the olive oil, and the salt, then add the remaining water and mix until a ball forms. Mix the dough for 2 minutes at low speed, 2 minutes at medium speed and 2 final minutes at low speed. Transfer the dough to a lightly oiled bowl, cover with plastic wrap, and let stand in a warm place until the dough has doubled in bulk, about 1 1/2 hours.
2. Put a pizza stone in the bottom of the oven and preheat the stone in the oven to 500 degrees F for about 45 minutes.
3. Punch down the dough and scrape it onto a floured work surface. Form the dough into a ball. Cut the ball into 8 equal-size pieces. Knead each piece into a ball and then flatten into disks. Cover with plastic wrap and let the dough rest for about 20 minutes.
4. Put the sun-dried tomatoes in a small saucepan and cover with water. Cover and simmer over low heat until very soft, about 5 minutes. Drain and coarsely chop the tomatoes. In a mini food processor, puree the chopped garlic with the olive oil.
5. Generously flour a pizza peel. Using a rolling pin, roll out a disk of dough to an 8-inch round, about 1/8 inch thick. (Alternatively, pull and stretch the disk into an 8-inch round.) Transfer the round to the peel and brush with the garlic puree. Scatter with one-eighth of the sun-dried tomatoes and arrange one-eighth of the sliced cheese on top. Drizzle with a little of the garlic puree and season with salt and pepper. Bake on the hot stone for about 4 minutes, until the crust is crisp and the cheese is bubbling. Top with some baby arugula and serve. Repeat with the remaining dough and toppings.

96. THREE CHEESE PESTO SPINACH FLATBREAD PIZZA

PREP TIME: 10 MINS

COOK TIME: 20 MINS

TOTAL TIME: 30 MINS

INGREDIENTS

- 1 [5 oz] box of spinach
- 1 TBSP butter
- 1 clove garlic, smashed and minced
- 1/4 cup heavy cream, room temperature
- 1/4 cup freshly grated parmesan cheese
- 1/8-1/4 tsp salt, to taste
- 1 garlic naan flatbread
- 2 oz mozzarella cheese, grated
- 2 tbsp feta cheese, crumbled
- 1-2 tsp pesto
- a pinch of red pepper flakes, for topping

DIRECTIONS:

1. Pre-heat oven to 350 degrees F.
2. Chop spinach and mince garlic.
3. Heat a deep pan to medium-high heat with 1 TBSP butter.
4. Add garlic and spinach and sauté until wilted.
5. Add heavy cream, parmesan, and salt and reduce heat to simmer, stirring frequently to thicken for about 5 minutes. Remove from heat and allow to cool slightly.
6. Spread spinach mixture onto your flatbread and top with mozzarella and feta cheese.
7. Drizzle with pesto and bake on a foil lined baking sheet at 350 for 12 min.
8. Change oven setting to broil for an additional minute or two, until golden and bubbly.
9. Top with red pepper flakes and enjoy!

NOTES

1. No fresh spinach? No problem! If you have creamed spinach squirreled away in your freezer it makes a fantastic base! Frozen chopped spinach will work too; simple squeeze it dry first and mix it with a dash of cream and a sprinkling of parm cheese. Whichever route you take, Popeye is sure to be proud!
2. To serve a crowd, this recipe easily doubles, triples, or quadruples. Have a quick and easy flatbread pizza party with friends or family and let everyone choose their toppings!

97. PIZZA ROLL-UPS

YIELDS: 1

INGREDIENTS

- 1 tube crescent rolls
- 1/4 c. marinara
- 1 c. shredded mozzarella
- 1/2 c. mini pepperoni

DIRECTIONS

1. Preheat oven to 350 degrees F. On a floured work surface, roll out crescent rolls into one large rectangle, pinching together seams.
2. Spoon marinara all over Crescent rectangle, then scatter with mozzarella and pepperoni.
3. Starting from the bottom, tightly roll up the rectangle like a cinnamon roll, then slice into four rolls. Transfer to a glass baking dish and bake until puffed and golden, 15 to 20 minutes.

98. MINI DEEP DISH PIZZAS

YIELD: 4 SERVINGS

PREP TIME: 15 MINUTES

COOK TIME: 10 MINUTES

TOTAL TIME: 25 MINUTES

INGREDIENTS:

- 4 "Old El Paso™ flour tortillas for burritos" (8 inch)
- 1 cup pizza sauce
- 3/4 cup shredded mozzarella cheese
- 1/4 cup freshly grated Parmesan
- 36 mini pepperonis

DIRECTIONS:

1. Preheat oven to 425 degrees F. Lightly oil a 12-cup muffin tin or coat with nonstick spray.
2. Working one at a time, lay tortilla on a flat surface. Using an empty can, cut 3-4 medium circles, pressing firmly enough in a rocking motion to cut through the tortilla.
3. Fit a tortilla circle into each of 12 muffin tins, pressing carefully to make sure there is an opening in the center. Scoop 1 tablespoon pizza sauce into each muffin tin. Sprinkle with mozzarella and Parmesan cheeses, topping with 3 mini pepperonis each.
4. Place into oven and bake for 10-12 minutes, or until cheese has melted.
5. Serve immediately.

99. GREEK PIZZA

INGREDIENTS

- 1 (16 oz) homemade or store bought pizza dough
- 2 1/2 Tbsp extra virgin olive oil , divided
- 3 garlic cloves , minced
- 1/2 tsp dried oregano
- 1/4 tsp dried basil
- 1/8 tsp dried thyme
- Salt and freshly ground black pepper
- 6 oz fresh mozzarella , chopped into pieces (regular low moisture mozzarella would be fine too)
- 4 oz feta , crumbled
- 1/2 cup chopped bell pepper (any variety)
- 1 cup diced grape tomatoes , halved
- 1/3 cup chopped kalamata or black olives
- 1/4 cup chopped red onion
- 1 Tbsp chopped fresh parsley

DIRECTIONS:

1. Preheat oven to 450 degrees. Place pizza stone in oven and rest 30 minutes. Meanwhile combine 1 1/2 Tbsp olive oil and garlic in a small bowl. Spread and shape pizza crust into a 12 - 13 inch round over a sheet of lightly floured parchment paper, while creating a rim along edge of dough. Brush pizza dough evenly with olive oil mixture. Sprinkle evenly with oregano, basil, thyme (leaving rim uncovered with herbs) and season lightly with salt and pepper. Top evenly with mozzarella and feta cheese. Bake in preheated oven 12 - 15 minutes until crust is golden.

Meanwhile, saute peppers in a skillet in 1 Tbsp olive oil over medium high heat until tender (you could also just add them on without sauteing).
2. Remove pizza from oven and immediately top with peppers, tomatoes, olives, onion and parsley. Cut into slices and serve.

100. SWEET POTATO, BALSAMIC ONION AND SOPPRESSATA PIZZA

YIELDS: 4

COOK TIME: 0 HOURS 30 MINS

TOTAL TIME: 0 HOURS 45 MINS

INGREDIENTS

- 1 tbsp. unsalted butter
- 1 tbsp. extra-virgin olive oil
- 1 large white onion
- 1 sprig oregano
- 1 tbsp. oregano leaves
- 1/4 c. balsamic vinegar
- 2 tbsp. balsamic vinegar
- kosher salt
- Freshly ground pepper
- 1 c. prepared mashed sweet potatoes
- 1 prebaked pizza crust
- 1 1/2 c. shredded mozzarella

- 4 oz. thinly sliced soppressata

DIRECTIONS

1. Preheat the oven to 450 degrees F. Set a pizza stone on the bottom of the oven (alternatively, the pizza can be baked directly on the oven rack). In a large skillet, melt the butter in the olive oil. Add the onion and oregano sprig, cover, and cook over moderately low heat, stirring occasionally, until softened, about 5 minutes. Add 2 tablespoons of water to the skillet and cook over moderate heat until the onion is caramelized, about 10 minutes; add a few tablespoons of water to the skillet if necessary. Add the balsamic vinegar and cook over moderate heat, stirring occasionally, until it has evaporated, about 10 minutes. Discard the oregano sprig and season the onion with salt and pepper.
2. Spread the sweet potatoes over the pizza crust. Top with the mozzarella, onion, and soppressata. Scatter the oregano leaves on top. Slide the pizza onto the stone and bake for about 10 minutes, until bubbling and golden in spots. Cut into wedges and serve.

101. THREE CHEESE PEACH AND PROSCIUTTO PIZZA WITH BASIL AND HONEY BALSAMIC REDUCTION

INGREDIENTS

- 1 (16 oz) pizza dough, homemade or store bought
- 1 Tbsp olive oil
- 1 clove garlic , finely minced
- Salt and freshly ground black pepper

- 3 oz prosciutto
- 4 oz ricotta cheese (1/2 cup)
- 5 oz fresh mozzarella, diced into small cubes
- 2 oz asiago cheese, shredded (1/2 cup)
- 1 1/2 medium fresh peaches
- 1 cup balsamic vinegar
- 1/4 cup honey
- Flour, for dusting
- 1/3 cup slightly packed fresh basil leaves, chopped

DIRECTIONS:

1. Place pizza stone in oven and preheat oven to 450 degrees. Let pizza stone preheat with oven and rest 30 minutes (assemble pizza during last 10 minutes or so).
2. Meanwhile, pour balsamic vinegar and honey into a large and deep skillet. Set skillet over medium heat, allow mixture to cook and simmer, until reduced to slightly under a 1/2 cup, about 15 minutes (I recommend using a silicone spatula to stir, so you can scrape bottom and sides of pan while stirring. Stir mixture occasionally during first 5 minutes, then stir constantly during last 10 minutes).
3. Lightly dust a sheet of parchment paper (about 14-inch long) with flour. Stretch and shape dough into a 12 1/2-inch round. In a small bowl, stir together olive oil and garlic. Brush mixture evenly over top of crust, working to evenly distribute garlic. Season crust lightly with salt and pepper. Layer prosciutto over crust into an even layer, aligning pieces side by side (if they overlap slightly that's fine). Dollop small portions of the ricotta over pizza, then sprinkles with mozzarella cubes and asiago cheese.
4. Cut peaches in half and core. Laying peaches with sliced side down, cut peaches into slices (slightly over 1/4-inch thick). Layer peaches evenly over pizza. Using a pizza peel, transfer pizza on parchment to preheated pizza stone in oven. Bake 10 - 12 minutes until edges are lightly golden.
5. Remove from oven, sprinkle with fresh basil, and drizzle with honey balsamic reduction (store left over reduction in fridge). Cut into slices and serve warm.

102. WHOLE-WHEAT PIZZA WITH ONIONS AND BITTER GREENS

YIELDS: 1

COOK TIME: 1 HOUR 0 MINS

TOTAL TIME: 2 HOURS 0 MINS

INGREDIENTS

- 3/4 tsp. active dry yeast
- 3/4 c. warm water
- 1/4 tsp. sugar
- 1 c. whole-wheat flour
- 1 c. all-purpose flour
- all-purpose flour
- 1/2 tsp. salt
- 2 1/2 tsp. extra-virgin olive oil
- extra-virgin olive oil
- 2 tbsp. canola oil
- 2 large onions
- 10 sprig thyme
- salt
- Freshly ground pepper
- 1/4 c. pine nuts

- 1 clove garlic
- 2 tbsp. extra-virgin olive oil
- 1 head radicchio
- 2 c. kale leaves
- 1 tbsp. sage leaves
- 5 oz. fresh mozzarella

DIRECTIONS

1. In the bowl of a standing electric mixer fitted with the dough hook, combine the yeast with 1/4 cup of the warm water and the sugar and let stand for 5 minutes. Add the remaining 1/2 cup of water, the whole-wheat and all-purpose flours, the salt, and the 2 1/2 teaspoons of olive oil and beat at medium speed until a soft, supple dough forms, about 8 minutes. Roll the dough into a ball, rub it with olive oil, and return it to the bowl. Cover the dough and let stand until doubled in bulk, about 1 hour.
2. Preheat the oven to 500 degrees F and place a pizza stone on the bottom rack of the oven, allowing at least 30 minutes for it to preheat. Punch down the dough and divide it into 3 pieces; form them into 3 balls and transfer to a lightly oiled baking sheet. Cover with oiled plastic wrap and let stand for 20 to 30 minutes.
3. In a large skillet, heat the canola oil. Add the onions and thyme and season with salt and pepper. Cover and cook over moderate heat, stirring once or twice, until the onions soften, about 5 minutes. Uncover and cook until the onions are very soft and golden, about 15 minutes longer; add water as needed to keep the onions from scorching. Discard the thyme.
4. Spread the pine nuts in a pie plate and toast in the oven until golden, 2 minutes.
5. In a large bowl, combine the garlic and olive oil. Add the radicchio, kale, and sage, season lightly with salt and pepper, and toss.
6. Turn the broiler on. Roll or stretch one ball of dough to a 10-inch round and transfer it to a floured pizza peel. Mound one-third of the greens on top, followed by one-third each of the onions, pine nuts, and cheese. Carefully slide the pizza onto the hot stone and bake until the crust is browned and the toppings are sizzling, 8 to 10 minutes. Cut the pizza into wedges and serve right away. Repeat to make the remaining 2 pizzas.

103. TURKISH GROUND-LAMB PIZZAS

YIELDS: 4

COOK TIME: 0 HOURS 40 MINS

TOTAL TIME: 1 HOUR 40 MINS

INGREDIENTS

- 1/2 tbsp. honey
- 1 tbsp. active dry yeast
- 1/2 tbsp. extra-virgin olive oil
- 1 c. whole wheat flour
- 1 c. all-purpose flour
- 1/2 tsp. salt
- 3/4 c. warm water
- 1 tbsp. extra-virgin olive oil
- olive oil
- 1 small onion
- 1 lb. ground lamb or beef
- 1 clove garlic
- salt
- Freshly ground pepper
- 1/4 c. oil-packed sun-dried tomatoes
- 1 tbsp. Turkish red pepper paste (see Note) or 2 jarred hot cherry peppers
- 1/2 tsp. ground cumin

- 4 large eggs
- 2 tbsp. flat-leaf parsley leaves

DIRECTIONS

1. In a small bowl, whisk the whole wheat flour with the all-purpose flour and salt. In a large bowl, combine the warm water and honey. Sprinkle the yeast over the water and let stand for about 5 minutes, until foamy. Stir in the olive oil and then the flour mixture. Gently knead the dough on a work surface until it forms a smooth, somewhat sticky ball. Lightly oil another bowl and add the dough. Cover with plastic wrap and let stand in a warm place until doubled in bulk, about 1 hour.
2. In a skillet, heat the 1 tablespoon of olive oil. Add the onion and cook over moderate heat until translucent, 4 minutes. Add the lamb and garlic and season with salt and pepper. Cook over moderately high heat, breaking up the meat with a wooden spoon, until the lamb is no longer pink, 3 minutes. Add the sun-dried tomatoes, red pepper paste, and cumin and cook, stirring, for 1 minute. Remove from the heat and season with salt and pepper.
3. Preheat the oven to 450 degrees F. Arrange oven racks on the top and bottom thirds of the oven. Preheat a large rimmed baking sheet in the oven for about 5 minutes.
4. On a lightly floured work surface, punch down the dough and cut into 4 pieces. Roll each piece into a 6-inch round. Arrange the dough rounds on the preheated baking sheet, about 1 inch apart. Bake on the bottom shelf of the oven for 2 minutes. Spread the lamb topping over the dough, leaving a 1/2-inch border around the edges; brush the borders with olive oil. Crack an egg in the center of each pizza (if using) and bake on the top shelf of the oven for about 6 minutes, until the crust is crisp on the bottom, the egg white is firm and the yolk is runny. Scatter the parsley over the pizzas and serve hot.

104. HUMMUS AND GRILLED-ZUCCHINI PIZZAS

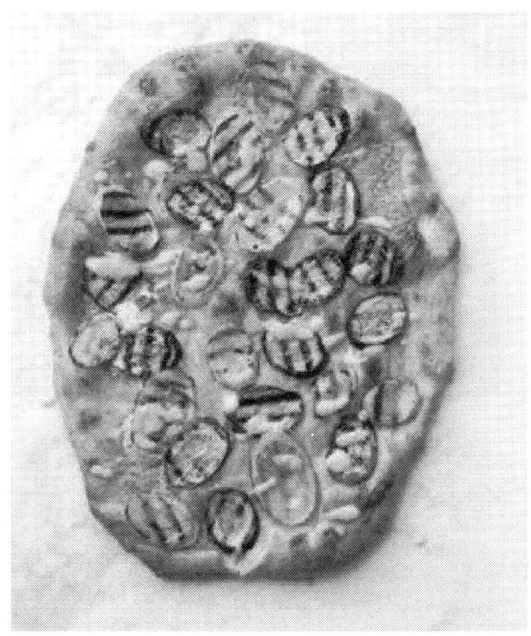

YIELDS: 1

COOK TIME: 0 HOURS 30 MINS

TOTAL TIME: 1 HOUR 0 MINS

INGREDIENTS

- 1 container roasted-garlic hummus
- 3/4 c. extra-virgin olive oil
- extra-virgin olive oil
- salt
- Freshly ground pepper
- 3 medium zucchini
- 16 oz. pizza dough

DIRECTIONS

1. Set a pizza stone in the oven and heat the oven to 500 degrees F for 30 minutes. Light a grill or preheat a grill pan. Scoop the garlic from the top of the hummus into a small bowl and stir in the 3/4 cup of olive oil. Season with salt and pepper. Transfer 3 tablespoons of the garlic oil to a large bowl. Add the zucchini and toss to coat. Whisk the hummus into the remaining garlic oil and season with salt and pepper.

2. Working in 2 batches, grill the zucchini slices over high heat until they are lightly charred, about 5 minutes. Brush the zucchini lightly with some of the hummus and grill for 1 minute longer, turning once.
3. Lightly rub 2 sheets of parchment paper with oil. Stretch each ball of pizza dough into a 12-inch round on each sheet. Brush each round with one-fourth of the hummus and top with the zucchini. Slide 1 parchment sheet onto the hot stone and bake the pizza for about 8 minutes, until the crust is browned. Transfer the pizza to a work surface and drizzle with some of the remaining hummus. Cut into slices and serve. Repeat with the remaining pizza.

Made in the USA
Middletown, DE
19 December 2018